IN THE THERAPIST'S CHAIR

In The Therapist's Chair

Dr. Jacqueline Simon Gunn

To order additional copies of this book, contact:
Xlibris Corporation
1-888-795-4274
www.Xlibris.com
Orders@Xlibris.com
78283

CONTENTS

To my father, Philip Simon, who has always had confidence in me and provided me an atmosphere of love and kindness in which to grow.

To my husband, Joseph Gunn, who always has faith in my professional endeavors.

And to my sister, Sharon Simon, who is one of the most unique people I know.

Preface

"Well-behaved women rarely make history!" This is the writing on a picture my mom brought back for me from a craft fair one day. "Well-behaved women rarely make history!" What a great line Laurel Thatcher Ulrich knew what she was talking about, and this is how my mother taught me to live my life. My mother taught me to pursue whatever I wanted, to be a strong, powerful woman who could accomplish anything I set my mind to and, most importantly, to be unafraid to be myself. She supported my decisions, even those that I don't think she always agreed with. This, in turn, taught me to trust myself and to feel secure, even if this meant doing things that weren't so conventional. If what I did expressed who I was, then that was fine with her. I think one of the most important things in life is to be true to yourself, whatever that means to you personally; my mother gave me the gift of knowing that this was the way to live.

My mother also taught me to find redeeming qualities in people. She taught me, by example, to notice what people give you rather than focusing on what they don't; because of this, I am able to find redeeming qualities in almost anyone. This is something I believe has made me so successful in my career as a psychologist. I can almost always find something attractive or positive in the people I meet and relate with. My mother taught me never to judge people by what they do or have done, but to treat all people with respect and admiration for their uniqueness as individuals; thanks to my mom, I do live my life this way.

I have accomplished quite a few magnificent things so far in my life, and I am sure there are many more to come. My mother was always there to support my accomplishments, even if it meant standing in a monsoon for four hours to watch me cross the finish line of a marathon. I know my mother was very proud of these things, but more importantly, she taught me that these accomplishments did not define who I was. I was perfect to her just by being myself: again, whatever that was, as long as it was a genuine expression of me. But outside of the things I have done, my mother taught me that life is a series of moments, and that some of the most important things we do as human beings are subtle and occur in a moment. Putting your hand on someone's shoulder when they need support is just as admirable and equally defining of your character as the big accomplishments you work toward. The subtle things we do or say define who we really are. My mother was truly gifted at this, and aside from the many magnificent grand accomplishments at which she succeeded, she knew the importance of subtlety. She gave more to people in these small moments than anyone I have ever known. I aspire to live this way, and it feels good to have internalized this quality from her.

My mother's way of living has been a great inspiration to me, and it certainly has influenced my approach to working with my patients. I wish she were here to read this book and to know that it was her way of living that afforded me the confidence to be true to my own unique self. I love you, Mom, and thank you.

In Loving Memory of My Mother, Rochelle Simon

Acknowledgments

Thank you to the whole *mishpacha*—my family and incredible support system. Thank you all for being uniquely yourselves. A special thanks to my friend Helene Pacifico, for encouraging me to pursue a career as a psychologist since we were children. Thank you to my supervisors and mentors, who always supported my endeavors and continue to keep my work exciting and challenging: Dr. Ken Winarick, Dr. Henry Paul, Dr. Janet Tintner and Martha Sermier. Thank you to my editors, Dr. Lia Kudless and Daryn Brown, who not only helped edit this book, but also encouraged me and gave me confidence throughout the entire process.

A special thanks to all the patients who inspired the writing of this book, and who add meaning to my life on a daily basis.

Introduction

Do not go where the path may lead. Go instead where there is no path and leave a trail.

—Ralph Waldo Emerson

The rainbow is more beautiful than the pot at the end of it, because the rainbow is now. And the pot never turns out to be quite what I expected.

—Hugh Prather, *Notes to Myself*

My patient and I were at a crossroads; we were stuck and unable to move the treatment forward. "What should I do?" I asked myself as I thought about the multiple alternative techniques I could try. I felt my patient's palpable pain as a result of his struggle; I decided to take a collaborative approach, asking, "How do you think I might best help you with your current circumstances?" He responded, "Just being with me and understanding my struggle is helpful. Everyone always tries to make you feel better by saying things that don't matter. You, you understand my pain, and that makes me feel less alone."

I knew then that my clinical role was just to sit with him in his current affect state and allow him to feel his emotions in a safe, contained, and empathic environment. This is not always easy, particularly for the neophyte therapist; we feel we should be "doing something something more active." However, by joining a patient in his or her psychological and emotional space, we *are* doing something, and in my clinical experience, eventually this moves the treatment and the therapeutic relationship forward.

Working as a clinician is one of the most exhilarating and intoxicating professions one can choose, but it is also quite complex and intricate. This book offers an intimate view into the experiential art of working clinically with patients in therapy. Using my own experiences as a clinical psychologist, I take personal journeys with six patients, each of whom offers something different towards the understanding of particular dynamics that may arise within a unique therapeutic dyad, and affords the reader valuable insight into the complicated dilemmas clinicians are exposed to on a daily basis. Other chapters, such as "Hugs and other forms of Personal Touch," specifically address predicaments that arise and unfold as part of the therapeutic process. These case studies and vignettes provide a private look into the mind of a therapist, and bring the therapeutic process to life.

Throughout my training, I have been influenced by many different theoretical orientations, and by a variety of professional experiences with well-experienced and seasoned supervisors. I have also learned a great deal from my personal experiences with each of my patients, who courageously and generously expose their inner selves, affording insight into the private workings of their hearts and minds.

This book might have been called *Establishing Uniqueness in the Therapeutic Encounter: My Approach to Psychotherapy in Clinical Practice.* Through my years of training, I have integrated these many influences and created my own unique and artful way of working with patients. I have been incredibly influenced by existential writings, both from philosophical and more dynamic psychological perspectives. Existentialism is essentially a psychology that focuses on the concerns inherent in human existence. The most common existential concerns are death, freedom, meaninglessness, and will. I was trained in phenomenology and ontology (the study of being), and have read widely in the field of philosophy. Having had most of my clinical training in psychodynamic theory and practice, I am a firm believer in the importance of the unconscious, defenses, cultural influences, and the relational process that occurs within the unique dyad. I find these four perspectives to work in conjunction with one another, and I integrate them in my approach. I believe the following case studies will illustrate how I navigate the terrain of each individual patient's psychology by integrating these techniques. I chose *In the Therapist's Chair* as my title because I feel this more closely embraces the fullness of the experiential nature I wish to convey to my readers.

One of the most vitally important perspectives in practicing psychology is the emphasis on treating each patient and therapeutic encounter as unique. Each person comes with his or her own novel perspectives, innate characteristics, personal histories, and modes of relating interpersonally. The reader is encouraged to suspend judgment and experience an open atmosphere where each patient expresses him or herself, in his or her own uniqueness, without presupposition. It is for these reasons that I have attempted to eliminate as much psychological jargon as possible and eradicate the use of diagnoses in my cases. It is not that I don't at times find diagnoses to be useful in conceptualizing and creating succinct ways of understanding patients; it is just that I find that they can limit our understanding of the full experiential nature of each unique patient.

Equally fundamental to my perspective is the art of working collaboratively with my patients. I often use the word "we" in my clinical work. It is my belief that this affords patients the opportunity to feel that they are active participants in their treatment, and facilitates a more comfortable and safe environment for more difficult material to arise and be expressed in the context of the therapeutic relationship.

I wrote this book primarily for the beginning therapist. However, I believe it will appeal to the more seasoned therapist and the layperson alike. It is a refreshingly honest look at the complexity of working as a clinician; additionally, it provides compelling stories of the psychology of the mind from the standpoint of both the patient and clinician.

Unless someone like you cares a whole awful lot, nothing is going to get better. It's not.

—Dr. Seuss, *The Lorax*

Chapter 1

Self-Acceptance Self-Exploration

The human individual, given a chance, tends to develop his particular human potentialities. He will develop then the unique alive forces of his real self: the clarity and depth of his own feelings, thoughts, wishes, interests; the ability to tap his own resources, the strength of his will power; the special capacities or gifts he may have; the faculty to express himself, and to relate himself to others with his spontaneous feelings.

—Karen Horney, *Neurosis and Human Growth*

A little over three years ago, I was referred a patient whom I still see. The referring clinician, who had met with the patient for just three sessions, informed me that the patient hadn't thought they were a good match the patient was not comfortable, and had asked to see someone else. The referring clinician characterized the patient as having "sexual issues" that were categorically pathological, and as she described the patient further, I could hear discomfort in the tone of her voice. The patient, A, was an artist, she explained, and had brought a collage of "pornographic pictures" into therapy. "Sounds interesting," I thought, and I agreed to accept the referral.

A arrived at our first session, and I comported myself with my usual openness and suspension of presupposition, disregarding the information I had received from the referring clinician. Within three sessions, it was clear to me and to A, who is very insightful, self-aware, and articulate, that when she feels uncomfortable she uses sex to unsettle the person with whom she is relating. A had been uncomfortable with her previous therapist; she described feeling judged, and felt that she was being negatively evaluated. "She was distant and just sat back and took notes," A stated, sounding irritated. We explored her propensity to use sex to disconcert others when she felt ill at ease. Within three months, A stopped using this self-preservation tactic in her outside life. I never did get to see the collage, which is a shame it sounded like an interesting piece of artwork.

When we live in the natural non-transcendental attitude, different thematic directions, and thus different directions of theoretical interest, open themselves to us in accord with the structure of the pre-given world the latter being given to us as our communal surrounding world. "Through this" means that the surrounding world is something changeable, that we progress in life, from one surrounding world to another, whereas throughout this alteration the same world is yet continuously experienced, the surrounding world becoming a manner of appearance of this world.

—Edmund Husserl, *The Crisis of European
Sciences and Transcendental Phenomenology*

As objective as we might like to be, all therapists live in the "pre-given" world, where, ostensibly, we cannot avoid our own conclusions and judgments. In our clinical work, it is important that we are consistently aware of our "natural attitudes," and that we do our best to defer such beliefs in the best interests of our patients. Patients need an environment of openness, unconditional acceptance, and suspended judgments in order to establish a therapeutic alliance and facilitate their own unique growth.

Unfortunately, even the *Diagnostic and Statistical Manual of Mental Disorders (DSM)* is predisposed to pathologize our patients, and in psychoanalytic circles it is often criticized for its categorical labeling system. It lumps clusters of personality traits, attitudes, and behaviors together, implying characterological patterns, and utilizes these so-called patterns to differentiate specific symptomologies and to indicate particular psychological disorders. More specifically, the criteria listed are considered overt manifestations of specific underlying behavioral dysfunctions, and are therefore used as diagnostic criteria.

Some argue that we as clinicians do need a sort of "cognitive toolbox" in order to conceptualize and classify certain symptoms that will inform our treatment; it is my approach that the classification system be used only as a supplement that should never diminish the importance of each patient's unique and distinctive qualities.

In order to be open and receptive to each patient's particular uniqueness, we need to be sufficiently accepting of ourselves. We need to be aware of our own unique traits, whether they elevate our feelings of self-worth or make us uncomfortable. Self-awareness, empathy, and acceptance of both our strengths and inadequacies are all vitally important to our work with our patients.

In my view, self-awareness is one of the most important prerequisites for becoming a successful clinician. It is important for two fundamentally related and not mutually exclusive reasons. First, we need to be very vigilant about what we bring to the co-created dyad; we need to have some sense of our own subjective realities, so that we do not impose our own biases on our patients. Second, we must realize that we are receptacles for our patients' unconscious feelings, thoughts, and fantasies. We need to be willing to explore our own affective states when sitting with a particular patient and be able to process what we are feeling; this provides invaluable information concerning our patient's internal world.

During supervision with one of my most self-aware and intuitive supervisees, we were processing her feelings about one of her patients. She was quite disconcerted and was having difficulty articulating her experience. "I feel uncomfortable. It is here," she said, as she motioned toward her stomach. It was clear that her discomfort was being evoked through the co-created dyad, because this supervisee does not usually feel this way when sitting with her patients. Through our concentrated exploration, we discovered that my supervisee was experiencing the patient's split-off and unconscious rage; this was valuable information, and provided insight into the patient's internal world of feelings that the patient had either blocked out of awareness or did not have the words to express.

Developing self-awareness is an ongoing and forever-evolving process, which can be greatly enhanced by therapy or analysis. Each moment of therapy with a patient is multifaceted and complex; we need to be attentive to the many different occurrences that take place during each session. One's own reactions and visceral experiences, as well as the patient's experiences and the content that he or she brings into the session, all need to be processed simultaneously. The clinician's insight, ability to negotiate these reactions and experiences, and proper timing of interventions (particularly interpretations), all comprise the art of psychotherapy and a successful therapeutic encounter.

Developing self-awareness and knowing oneself is also fundamental to establishing a professional identity. It is only through this process that we can engage spontaneously and genuinely with our patients and such genuine engagement correlates directly with successful treatment outcomes. Patients don't want to feel that they are being analyzed via textbook knowledge; they want to feel genuine collaborative relationships with their therapists.

I remember my internship. I started out feeling relatively confident and competent in proportion to my experience level. However, when I was first exposed to multiple and divergent supervisory perspectives, I found myself engrossed in internal neurotic dialogues whenever I was with a patient. I would think, "So-and-so said I should do *this*. No. So-and-so said I should do *that*." I felt that I had lost my natural ability to use my own intuition and my unique personal style, which was based on who I was characterologically. I finally became able to integrate what I had learned from my supervisors with my own unique way of relating in the year following my internship. This is the laborious and often painful process of establishing a professional identity: we must be honest with ourselves about who we are in order to resolve this conflict successfully.

We must also be acutely aware of the "now" why, in a particular moment, does certain material come up or show itself in the therapy room? Sometimes timing is everything. For example, patient H. I had been seeing H for about four months. He had come to therapy suffering from dysphoric mood and anxiety secondary to relationship difficulties with his girlfriend of three years. I had the sense that what was going on for him was far more complicated, but he held steadfast to his presenting complaint. As the season changed from winter to spring, he came into session one afternoon wearing shorts. Mid-session, I happened to notice that his legs were shaved. I also noticed that I reacted viscerally to what I witnessed; I felt uncomfortable, as though the hairs on my back (if I have any) were standing up. In that moment, H shared that he really wanted to be a woman, as the intonation of his voice and his body language became more feminine. Quelling the many exploratory questions I immediately had, I wondered with him, "Why now? Why after four months did you finally decide to share this?" He explained that it was only through our four months of therapy that he had become able to fully recognize and put words to his true desire.

Chapter 2

"My Heart Felt Broken"

People who feel empty never heal by merging with another incomplete person. On the contrary, two broken-winged birds coupled into one make for clumsy flight. No amount of patience will help it fly; and ultimately each must be pried from the other and wounds separately splinted.

—Irvin Yalom, *Existential Psychotherapy*

S came into therapy following the breakup of a six-year on-again, off-again relationship. I could hear the crisis in her voice as we set up our first appointment over the phone. So I wasn't surprised when she began our first session by hysterically crying from the moment she stepped into my office. My immediate sense was that S was frantic, and, for the moment, uncontrollable and inconsolable. I sat with her in her brokenhearted, grief-stricken state for at least five minutes until she started to calm down. Once she regained her composure, S looked up, making eye contact for the first time, and instantly apologized for crying. I acknowledged her apology with a nod of recognition and empathically remarked, "You are really suffering." Tears were still in her eyes, but she seemed more in control now.

This is how our treatment together began. S and I worked in therapy together twice a week for six years with a two-month break in between. I learned in the first session that S was in the grueling process of trying to separate from a man she had been involved with "on and off" for six years. S revealed that she had a pattern of becoming involved with emotionally unavailable men from whom she could not separate, despite the destructive nature of the relationships. "This last one really did me in," S stated, and said she was coming to therapy to try to understand what perpetuated her pattern.

I had many questions for S, but I could feel the pressure of her need to process her present predicament, so I decided to start with this. As I encouraged her to elaborate on her current relationship, it seemed as if it wasn't much of an intimate relationship at all. Still tearful, S shared that she had been seeing D for six years. The condition of their relationship throughout had consisted of S's pursuing D and persuading him to spend time with her. D would come over once or twice a week, although his visits had lessened within the last year, and they would have wine or dinner and then sex. D would sometimes spend the night only to arise early and leave abruptly, or he would run off shortly after sex. Occasionally, they would go out for dinner or drinks prior to sex, but D never spent holidays with S, he didn't indulge her with gifts, and his compliments were limited to admiring her body. There was some nonsexual intimacy, such as cuddling following sex, but this lasted for only a brief time prior to D's falling asleep or leaving with an excuse about why he needed to go home.

Between their liaisons, they exchanged e-mails, text messages, and an occasional phone call. The content of their communication usually involved sex talk or simply making plans for their next rendezvous. S felt extremely unsatisfied throughout the relationship and tried relentlessly to end it, only to return to D after a short separation. I was curious and asked, "Do you have a sense of what makes you go back?" S remarked that she usually called D when she felt lonely or was feeling badly about herself. I had many hypotheses already, but S's desperation was palpable and filled the room, so I knew I had to tread lightly.

At the close of this first session, which was difficult for me to end, I could feel S's turmoil. She remarked that she felt a little better just having had a place to talk about her excruciating pain. We scheduled another appointment for just two days later. Between these two sessions, I thought about S quite a bit. The potency of her conflict really affected me, and I wondered why. I realized the morning of our next session that I felt like S was screaming, "Please help me! I don't have the strength to help myself."

S arrived at our second session with the same intensity. She continued, tearfully, to discuss her relationship with D. She spent most of the session sobbing while describing in detail the ultimate demise of their relationship. She described the last six months as "torturous," as D continued to pull back from her to the extent that he often would not even respond to her text messages. When S confronted D about why he was distancing himself from her, he denied that anything was different, and then he pulled away even more. S, feeling desperate, distraught, and "out of her mind," started driving by D's apartment trying to figure out what he was doing. She stated, "I just wanted to know what was going on. It was driving me crazy."

S and D had never discussed the extent of their commitment. When feeling abandoned and dismissed by D, S described having sex with other men and occasionally with women. She even carried on other semi-relationships with other men, hoping that she would meet someone more appropriate, who might help her get over D. In spite of this, S described "freaking out" one night when she saw D kissing another woman in front of his apartment. "Freaking out?" I inquired. S stated that she had gotten out of her car, walked right over to D and this other woman, and confronted D about his disappearance. S, so ashamed that she couldn't even make eye contact with me towards the end of the story, stated that D had walked her back to her car, escorted her in, and abruptly and forcefully said he would call her the next day. He didn't. S hadn't heard from him since, nor would he respond to any of her attempts to contact him. It had been three weeks.

We had about eight minutes left until the session's end, and S began sobbing. "What's wrong with me?" she asked. "Why do men always leave me? Why does this always happen?" Since we were near the session's close, I needed to contain her affect enough that I felt she would be able to leave the session without falling apart afterward. I acknowledged her sadness and desperation, and affirmed that what she had gone through sounded awful and traumatic. Then we discussed how we were going to work together to help her feel better. S calmed down, although she was still a bit weepy, and said she felt comfortable enough to leave the session. I sensed that S wouldn't unravel, and that it was safe for her to leave, but I did wonder where she planned to go after session. She was going to her studio. She was an artist.

A great many patients come into treatment in crisis, and it is vitally important for clinicians to bear witness to and process the crisis before moving the therapy forward. Gathering historical information is essential, and is the framework from which we can begin to conceptualize and understand each patient's uniqueness. This, in my experience, will evolve naturally, as the therapeutic relationship unfolds and the crisis begins to subside.

S spent many of our early sessions focused on D. It was particularly difficult for S to move past her ruminations, because she was lost and confused about why D had pulled away. She would still try to contact him, usually via e-mail, at least once a week, seeking an answer. Her efforts to connect with him left her feeling simultaneously ashamed and "weak," as it was clear that D did not wish to speak with her. His abrupt rejection at the end of the relationship grossly affected S's already low self-worth. Paradoxically, as I will explain later, S's low self-worth was one of the fundamental reasons that she continued to reach out. Without D's acceptance, S felt worthless, empty, and unlovable. This was the core of S's view of herself, and working through and understanding the origin of these painful feelings would eventually become a crucial part of our work together.

The sadness and despair Polly feels when she looks at herself in the mirror or thinks about her personal characteristics is assumed to be genetically related to similar feelings experienced when her parents, the original mirror of the developing self, showed little evidence that Polly was pleasing to them.

—Susan Miller, *The Case of Polly, from The Shame Experience*

S's deep-rooted sense of worthlessness and self-scrutiny was painful to sit with and quite incongruent with the way I experienced her. S was thirty-six. She had long blonde hair that flawlessly framed her face, bright beautiful skin, soft brown almond-shaped eyes, and the most fabulous tone of voice I had ever heard. She was an exceptionally talented sculptor and painter, she comported herself with class, was highly intelligent and interesting, was deeply concerned for others, and reflected a deep appreciation for aesthetics. As our therapeutic relationship evolved, I found S a pleasure to work with and, in one word, lovely.

S continued to be consumed by thoughts of D and the multiple unanswered questions surrounding their relationship. As treatment unfolded, she was slowly able to concentrate on other clinically relevant topics aside from D. I learned that S had two elder sisters and a younger brother. She was raised in a small rural town in upstate New York. Her parents were still together, but S described their relationship as estranged. She had no active memories of any affection between her parents. As she continued to describe the atmosphere in which she was raised, I began to have images of S's family as multiple strangers living in a house where all they shared was a roof and some walls. I sensed a real disconnectedness among them through S's descriptions of their ways of relating to one another.

S's parents both worked when she was growing up, and she often came home to an empty house. She described much of her childhood as lonely, and depicted herself as the artist of the house a child whose primary relationship was with her canvas and paints. S did not experience any overt abuse growing up, but she did often feel neglected and emotionally abandoned by her parents. She described having relationships with her siblings, particularly her sister, who was ten years her senior. However, she illustrated these relationships as contentious and conflict ridden even in the present.

S expressed one noteworthy experience that she felt truly exemplified her solitude. One afternoon when S was twelve, she was at a friend's house. She went upstairs to use the bathroom, and, to her dismay, saw blood on her underwear. S, never having been told about menstruation, was shocked and panicked. She yelled for her friend, and her friend's mother benevolently explained to S what the blood was. When I empathically was curious about what this experience had been like for her, she expressed some anger, but feeling ashamed was what S remembered most. My heart felt broken upon hearing this story, and the feeling stayed with me for the rest of the day.

S also described being criticized for wanting to pursue a career in art. Her other siblings' endeavors were more acceptable in S's parents' minds; they were going into teaching, nursing, and business, and these were "more solid" careers, S's father emphatically argued. In fact, S had been artistic from the time she was a young child, and her parents had always discouraged her from any artistic interests. This left S feeling rejected at the very core of her being, as she would later tearfully articulate. S did not describe art as an activity in which she participated, but rather stated, "Art is who I am." This declaration made it abundantly clear that something so central to S's identity and perceived real self was not only being undermined, but also out-rightly rejected. This was a breeding ground for developing alienation from one's real and genuine self. How, I wondered, did S defy these challenges to the core of her being and remain true to her inner self? How tragic it would be if she were unable to overcome these parental ideals. I also believed that this was the origin of S's self-hatred, but recognized that it was too soon in our therapeutic process to share this hypothesis.

There is more of him in that front stoop than in all the sales he ever made.

—Arthur Miller, *Death of a Salesman*

Now having a plethora of information regarding S's childhood experiences, I began to formulate hypotheses regarding her interpersonal difficulties with men. Needing more information about her relationship history before I could perform any interpretive interventions, I began to explore S's other relationships with men. "You indicated, at the beginning of our work together, that what happened to you with D happens all the time. Can you tell me more about that?" I curiously inquired.

S and I spent many months exploring her history of intimate and sexual relationships with men. Intrusive and painful thoughts surrounding D's complete disappearance and dismissal still arose intermittently throughout these months. It became abundantly clear through our exploration that S suffered from tremendous self-hatred and worthlessness, which originated from early rejections of her true self and from an environment that did not foster S's unique and extraordinary qualities as an individual. Feeling that S was not emotionally ready to address her underlying self-hatred and its ultimate impact on her life, I held back and waited for the timing to be right; a premature interpretation for someone like S could damage our alliance and ultimately result in her leaving treatment.

S described a long-standing history of relationships with men that were indeed quite similar to her relationship with D. One outstanding quality was that she was often attracted to and became involved with men who, unlike D, came on very strong in the beginning. S would often spend hours on the phone with these men, including internet dates whom she had not yet met, discussing their excitement about the possibility of an emerging relationship. Strikingly, many of these conversations would ultimately become sexual in nature soon after the typical "get to know you" formalities. When I was curious about S's feelings about these conversations, she shared that she found the sex talk exciting and exhilarating. She was beginning to wonder if this was problematic. "Okay, good," I thought privately. "She's becoming curious about her relational style."

Sometimes, S shared, she would meet these men and would have a great time and incredible sex. She would be filled with enthusiasm and promise, only to be disappointed when they later communicated that they weren't interested. S described anger towards these men, but she was usually resilient enough to recover from the rejections quickly. However, when a few experiences such as these would happen in succession, she would become dysphoric and again begin to feel worthless and unlovable. I associated the experiences that S described with a roller coaster. She diverted eye contact for a moment, and then emphatically and tearfully stated, "It is!"

S began to disclose her experiences in a few longer-term, more-significant relationships. Through S's narrative, I noticed that in these situations, the men would come on strong, mostly with words, only to start distancing themselves as soon as any relationship-like need was placed on them. In these instances, S would feel frenzied and frantic as she felt them pulling away. She also described bewilderment and confusion surrounding what she experienced as a quite perplexing situation. To S, things seemed to going well, and she could not understand what was happening in these relationships.

As S exposed her feelings and her confusion to me, her speech accelerated and became more pressured. In beginning to open up the relational space, I noticed with S the changes in her speech, and I wondered what she was feeling in the room as she was sharing this intimate material with me. S was able to articulate her feelings of desperation and the concomitant humiliation that resulted from continually finding herself in these situations. I could feel her self-hatred and feelings of abandonment permeating the room. These feelings, sadly, organized her core self and her identity, and she could not at this point in treatment find words for them.

We were now at the beginning of our second year of treatment, and I started to process internally the ways that S related to me. She was a very engaged patient, which was surprising, given the atmosphere in which she grew up and the relationship history she had described to me. As an experienced clinician, I knew I had to use the therapeutic relationship to better understand her specific relational style, if I was going to be able to help her with what I had come to understand as her problems with intimacy. Clearly, from S's description of her intimate relationships with men, she had the propensity to overestimate the intimacy she engaged in. What S experienced as intimate relationships, were, in fact, primarily based on good times and sex. I needed to explore this with S, as well as the way in which she experienced our relationship, if treatment were to move forward.

As a clinician, it is quite unusual for me not to have an intuitive sense of the patient's experience of me in the therapy room. I noticed that despite our good rapport and S's seeming engagement with me, I did not feel anything remarkable. I felt empathy and warmth toward S, and I really enjoyed working with her; however, there was something profoundly missing, and this absence was important clinical information.

Intimate relationships are the bête noire for the person with an impaired real self, calling as they do for self-expression, self-revelation, and the ability to function independently while sharing with another human being.

—James F. Materson, *The Search for the Real Self*

I was looking for a window through which to begin processing how S experienced our relationship, when she came in with the following dream:

> *I was in the local bar across the street from my apartment,*
> *but it looked different. Instead of bar stools, there were couches*
> *to sit on. I was by myself, and felt lonely. Then a woman walked*
> *in. She looked like you. She reminded me of you, but it wasn't*
> *you. She came over to me. At first we were sitting on couches*
> *across from each other just talking. I liked her; she was a good*
> *listener. I moved over to her couch, and we began kissing and*
> *fondling each other. It felt weird at first, but then it felt really*
> *good. I woke up, and I was wet down there.*

What an intriguing and telling dream, I thought, as associations ran excitedly through my head. Dreams can provide a great deal of clinical information that a patient often cannot allow into waking awareness. I asked S for her associations with the dream. She was having some difficulty making sense of it, and I hypothesized that this difficulty had to do with the dream's intimate content. Through a more direct inquiry, I aided her a bit, asking, "What do the couches remind you of or make you think of?" S was able to make the association between the couches in the bar, and the couch she sat on every week in my office, directly across from me. "The woman, it was you? No, it wasn't, was it?" S struggled.

It took all my internal resources to hold myself back from interpreting the dream for her. It was just so apparently evocative. I wanted her to make her own associations, so that we could process the meaning collaboratively. "Think of the dream as a metaphor. What would it mean if the woman *was* me?" I pushed a bit, but I felt that S was curious and ready for the challenge. "Well, I feel close to you, and I find you attractive, but no offense, I don't want to have sex with you," S said, preserving the sanctity of our relationship. She continued then to describe her inclination to be sexually attracted to women, and revealed that she had had some sexual experiences with them. "Do you feel close to them? Is there any emotional intimacy there?" I queried. S described her experiences with women as either friendly or purely sexual.

S really wanted to know what I thought of the dream. "Isn't it your job to interpret the dream?" she persisted. I wasn't sure until later if I had made the right decision to interpret the dream for her. I just couldn't help myself; it contained too much important clinical material, and her unconscious mind, via the dream, communicated a readiness to begin working on some more intense clinical material.

With some hesitation, I began to interpret that the dream indicated to me that S was confusing the shared intimacy and closeness she felt from our therapeutic relationship with desires to be sexual. I continued by connecting this to her overall way of confusing intimacy with sex; this, I furthered, was similar to the way she experienced intimacy with the men with whom she became involved. S, never having experienced healthy intimacy in her relationships with her parental figures, was unable to experience true closeness it was foreign, unfamiliar, and uncomfortable. This is quite common for someone who had been deprived of the intimate parent-child connection while growing up. Therefore, S's resolution, although it caused her anguish, was that she only was able to understand closeness if it included a sexual component.

S's relationship with me offered her a new way of relating; as a result of the boundaries of the therapeutic frame, she experienced shared intimacy without sex. This felt good, but was also somewhat disorienting and confusing, as she had never had this experience before. S sat in amazement, and I knew then that I had made the right decision to interpret the dream for her. S stated, "I never thought of it that way, but it makes complete sense. Thank you, Jacquie." This, in fact, opened up the therapy and created space in the room to begin to process deeper and more difficult, albeit necessary, material, so that S might find a more constructive resolution to her conflicts and slowly build her self-worth.

We spent months working collaboratively on S's inclination to sexualize her romantic relationships as a way to defend against genuine intimacy. We also explored her underlying feelings of worthlessness and alienation from her real self. It became clear to S that her parents had never encouraged any of her interests as a child, but rather had dissuaded her from pursuing any of her childhood dreams or endeavors, particularly her artwork. Despite her ability to fulfill her dream of living independently as an artist, S never received any positive affirmation from her parents or siblings. In fact, no one in her family showed any interest in her art; they never even came to any of her openings.

S knew she was a talented artist, but without any acknowledgment from her parents, she sometimes felt alienated from this fundamental part of herself; she even felt, at times, that her life as an artist lacked any meaning. We were working hard in therapy to help S independently gain the meaning she so greatly needed; S needed to separate from her parents' rejections, which she had internalized, by creating an integrated sense of meaning on her own. S started to bring in photos of some her work to show me. I always acknowledged her talents and encouraged her to pursue her goals; she was clearly quite talented and special. Over time, my genuine interest seemed to help S integrate the split-off parts of herself, and to eventually gain confidence in herself as a successful artist.

S began to express newfound feelings of independence and confidence. It was clear from the feeling in the room that S was doing a lot better. She decided to start dating again. S, now almost thirty-nine, really wanted to meet a man and start a relationship. I wanted S to date, and even encouraged her to do so, but I sensed that she was still vulnerable to choosing a man who was unavailable. She had made tremendous strides in treatment, but I still sensed ambivalence surrounding her ability to engage truly with someone on an intimate level; her sense of self was still quite tenuous, and I feared she could easily lose herself once involved with a man. I shared my trepidation with her, and we decided that we would use her dates as clinical material.

We were in our third year of therapy together, and S began opening up about her discomfort with her body and her on-and-off tendency to binge. I, of course, thought, "Why now? Why, after three years together, did S decide to bring this in the room at this moment?" S described vacillating thoughts about her body; sometimes she was comfortable with it, and other times she despised it. She also stated that she really hadn't binged in at least a year, but had done so the past few nights. She thought it was time to bring it up in therapy, particularly since she was going to start dating again.

There were many thoughts running through my mind and many directions I could have gone with this material. I believed these disclosures actually were related to S's decision to start dating again, but I held off on this thought. Instead, I decided to begin by exploring S's experience of her body. S had a very curvaceous body, but she saw herself as overweight, and felt that this was why men often didn't want to see her again after sex. I took her lead. "Sounds like this may be coming up now in response to anxiety you are having as a result of your decision to start dating," I offered. S became tearful and admitted that this had always been an issue for her when it came to dating. S revealed that she imagined that men want a "tall, thin woman," and this, she was not. She described apprehension prior to her Internet dates; S believed that once these men saw her body they would be either disinterested or interested only in sex. Over numerous sessions, we discussed that each man has his own ideas of physical attractiveness. We ultimately came to understand S's intermittent disgust with her body as a concretization of her internal self-hatred. Her fears of being rejected had more to do with the experience of feeling unimportant and unlovable than it did with how she felt about her body.

Through the lens of phenomenology, the mind and body are seen as one. In fact, early phenomenological writing argues that classical psychoanalysis, particularly instinct theories, separate the mind and body, and that early instinct theories don't account for the impact the patient's world—the zeitgeist—has on his or her presentation and symptom formation. I believe these theoretical disparities are semantic more than anything else. Contemporary psychoanalytic thinking has integrated early phenomenological philosophies in the understanding of the patient and techniques of treatment. In my conceptualization and treatment of patients, I perceive the mind and body as one. I have experienced, with each of my patients, how the body often communicates what the conscious mind is unable to know. Understanding the body as a metaphor for these unknowns provides vital clinical material, and often results in abatement and relief of painful symptoms.

To venture causes anxiety, but not to venture is to lose one's self. And to venture in the highest sense is precisely to be conscious of one's self.

—Søren Kierkegaard

For S, understanding her negative body image as a metaphor for her more encompassing self-hatred did help her to integrate her experience of her body with painful cognitions surrounding her sense of self. She reported a newfound comfort with her body, and even described feeling "proud" of it. As treatment went on and S began dating, it became amply clear that the way she felt about her own body translated directly to the acceptance or rejection she received from men. Her feelings about her body, and therefore the confidence level she exuded while on her dates, communicated self-love or self-hatred, as well as the level of her dependency on others' assessments to distinguish her own affect state.

I inquired now about S's bingeing. She described bingeing on and off throughout her life. She stated that her entire family was overweight, and she believed that this had to do with their using food as a way to cope. I believed that S had developed an intimate relationship with food as a result of the complete lack of relatedness she had experienced in her home growing up, but I kept this to myself, because I knew it would unfold later at a more appropriate time. I encouraged S to be vigilant and to write down her feelings prior to her binges, so that we might be able to establish a pattern and particular triggers. When not binging, S described eating very healthily and going to the gym three to four times a week.

S came into the next session and reported that she believed her three-day binge was related to returning ruminations about D and the end of their relationship. She had begun communicating with a few different men on the Internet, and was excited, despite her anxiety about dating; her anxiety was manageable and very appropriate, given the circumstances and where we were in treatment. S tearfully expressed re-experiencing some of her painful feelings surrounding the end of the relationship with D. She shared fears of possibly being hurt again. I could really feel her fearfulness, and I felt like I just wanted to hug her and console her. I decided, after some thought, to share this with her, and S began sobbing. "I feel like I need a hug. No one has ever known what I needed before." In that moment, I could feel the strength of our growing intimacy. I was so moved I could feel my eyes welling up with tears. Thankfully, I was able to remain contained.

In spite of her fears, S began dating. We spent many months focused on the many encounters she had with men. It was clear that S's mood and her propensity to binge was directly related to her dating experiences. S would become very excited and enthusiastic when she met someone and, as I anticipated, would often lose herself in the fantasies about their future as early as the first date. Simultaneously, she would become distraught when the relationship did not progress. I gently encouraged S to be curious about the intensity of her reactions. Eventually, after many sessions and many failed dates, S became aware of how emotionally dependent she was on these men men who, in reality, she didn't even really know and for the most part weren't right for her.

We explored how, sadly, her dependency needs were not met when she was a child, and having these needs met in childhood is a prerequisite to establishing a secure independent identity as an adult a sense of self strong enough to stand alone. This sense of self, in turn, is essential for developing the abilities to choose an appropriate mate, tolerate the anxiety of the early stages of a relationship, and ultimately sustain a loving relationship without losing one's self. S continued dating, but now, after our many months of work towards securing her independent identity and real self, she was very conscious of her responses to men. She was even able to contain fantasies about them and slowly let them reveal who they were. In short, S was more able to make appropriate decisions about with whom she would be involved. I could feel the difference in S, and even noticed it in her overall cadence and in the way she related to me.

We were at the beginning of our fifth year of treatment when I took a two-week vacation abroad. Although I had a covering psychologist, as I always do, it was the first time I had gone away for two weeks in a row and was unreachable. During our first session following my return, S reported the following dream:

> *I came to session one afternoon for our scheduled appointment, and you weren't there. I didn't know where you went, and I had no way to reach you. I called your cell phone many times, but it was turned off. I started bingeing and couldn't stop. I was really angry.*

Patients always have feelings about and reactions to our vacations, some more obvious than others. When I had probed S for feelings about my two-week break prior to my departure, she said she would be fine, and would not even take the covering psychologist's contact information without some cajoling on my part. This dream not only conveyed the impact my vacation had had on S, but also made apparent to her, for the first time, just how dependent she had become on our relationship.

When I probed S for feelings and associations to her dream, she began sobbing. She described feeling lost while I was away. She further described, with anger and discomfort, how angry she was that I went away. She was very uncomfortable with how dependent she had become on me. Like me, S hadn't realized the strength of her dependency until I was unavailable. This simultaneously scared and angered her. S was extremely angry; I tried to contain her, but was unsuccessful. She stormed out ten minutes before the session was over, declaring, "I need a break from therapy. I need something else, something I can depend on all the time!"

I thought that S was just reacting in the moment, but when I called her the following day, she insisted that she needed some time and would call me if she wanted to return to therapy. I tried to have her in for one more session to process her feelings, but she was firm in her decision. I was at a loss; I felt abandoned by S, and guilty for going on a vacation, which, rationally, I knew I deserved. I imagined that the abandonment I felt was at least partially a projection of S's feelings of abandonment. I wanted to call her again, but I knew this wasn't the right thing; in fact, it was possible that my desire to call her was also a projection of S's historical reaction to abandonment that I wanted to reach out to an unwilling partner in a relationship, just as S, at the beginning of our work together, had continued to inappropriately pursue the men she felt had abruptly terminated relationships with her. A phone call would meet my needs, but was not in S's best interest or in the best interest of the therapeutic relationship. So I held off, hoping that now she had the resources to process her feelings on her own and eventually return to therapy.

Exactly two months later, I received a phone call from S asking for an appointment. She was ready to resume treatment. I was relieved and delighted to hear from S, but also anxious. During our two-month separation, I had become engaged and now wore an engagement ring. Responding to patients' personal questions is a delicate issue that requires special and multifaceted consideration. The situation becomes even more complex when there is physical evidence of a change in one's personal circumstances, such as an engagement ring. In therapy, I decide how to respond to personal questions from my patients on an individual basis, and thoughtfully consider each unique dyad.

I realized that I was particularly uneasy about S's noticing my ring. In fact, when she came in for our first session, and for many sessions to follow, I turned the ring around so that the diamond was hidden, hoping to make it less obvious. I realized, after some contemplation, that I imagined that S had assumed I was also single, and that she thought I could really understand her struggles, as a kindred spirit. I was afraid for her to know the truth about my personal relationship; I imagined this knowledge would alter our alliance and make it more difficult for her to expose her shame to me. Interestingly, S did not seem to notice the ring for quite a few months. I believe that she also did not want to rupture our alliance by experiencing me as someone capable of having what she wanted; she did not want to envy me.

S came to our first session with some valuable insight. She described feeling so overwhelmed by her growing dependence on me and her concomitant fears that I would disappoint or leave her that she needed to separate for a short time to reestablish a sense of independence. We discussed her progress, and her growing awareness of some of the conflicts that made her ability to be truly intimate quite difficult. The fact that S had left and then come back, and her ability to process and articulate this experience, signified tremendous progress and indicated that she was integrating once-alienated parts of herself. This integration and acceptance of her dependence implied a greater ability to interact as a whole person in a healthy relationship.

S continued dating, and we continued to evaluate her experiences with the different men she encountered. She often would bring in e-mails or long back-and-forth text messages wondering if I noticed any "red flags." I always read what she brought in, but instead of providing her with answers,

I encouraged her to be curious about what she thought or imagined. I was working hard to foster S's independence by being an available support while simultaneously demonstrating to her that I had faith in her ability to make her own decisions. I was communicating through my action, or inaction, that I experienced S as the strong, independent woman she was; I just needed her to integrate this into her own experience of herself.

S was really making progress as we began our sixth year of treatment together. It had been six months since her last binge. She was now able to recognize and articulate how her relationship with food related to her fear of relating to others, particularly men. Now feeling more secure and independent, she was able to sit with her feelings of self-hatred when they emerged (though they were coming up less and less), without using food to soothe herself. It was at around this time that S became involved with a man, P.

Uncharacteristically, she allowed the relationship to evolve slowly, and waited for P to earn her trust and show her that he was worthy of her affection. As their relationship progressed and it became apparent that it might lead somewhere, S noticed my engagement ring for the first time. "You're engaged?" she asked, astonished. "Is it recent? I never noticed your ring before. Wow, it's beautiful," she said with amazement. I disclosed that I had been engaged since she had returned to treatment. We explored together how she was only able to take in the ring and acknowledge that I maintained a personal relationship outside of our therapeutic dyad once she felt secure in her own relationship.

S moved in with P about five months into their relationship. She was finally able to remain independent and maintain her sense of self while sharing her life with a man. I was overjoyed. She was no longer a *broken-winged bird*, and she was ready to fly freely.

The demands of intimacy require, at once, being an individual and, paradoxically, joining with someone else.

—Donald Dutton, *The Batterer*

S decided to terminate treatment a few months later. She felt that she had developed the resources she needed to move ahead with her life and make appropriate and constructive choices. During our two-month termination process, she did express sadness surrounding the loss of our relationship, but understood that the boundaries of therapy did not allow for ongoing contact. We did leave an opening for her to return to treatment at any time. I felt a sense of longing and profound sadness as I watched S leave my office for the last time. We had shared so much during the six years we had worked together. I had watched her grow into the strong, independent woman that I had always known she was.

Chapter 3

"Can I Live in the Castle and Wait for my Prince?"

We put thirty spokes to make a wheel; but it is on the hole of the center that the use of the cart hinges.
We make a vessel from a lump of clay; but it is the empty space within the vessel that makes it useful.
We make doors and windows for a room; but it is the empty spaces that make the room livable.
Thus, while existence has advantages, it is the emptiness that makes it useful.

—Lao Tzu, *Tao Teh Ching*

C provoked me. She challenged my ability to contain my own feelings, she made me question my talents as a clinician, she behaved as though she were entitled, and she attempted to cross boundaries that most patients wouldn't think of crossing. And yet, she was wonderful, kind, and delightful.

C was in therapy to deal with dysphoric feelings resulting from her extremely tumultuous romantic relationship. She arrived at our first session on time, which I would quickly discover was an anomaly. I could sense her anxiety immediately and intensely while she decided where to sit. She had a choice between the patients' chair, which was quite close to me, and the more-comfortable couch, slightly farther away. I observed her quandary, but said nothing. C finally decided to sit on the couch. This was the beginning of our six years of weekly treatment together.

C was clearly distraught as she began to provide me with the details of her extremely abusive relationship. Her overall presentation was frantic, which I sensed had to do with fears of abandonment. I had many questions, but it was clear that she needed to talk, and my inquiries may have been intrusive. So I listened attentively to her story, responding only with empathic and validating statements.

C had been involved with D for the past five years. D lived in France, where he was born and raised. They had met while C was on a vacation, and, according to C, they instantly "fell in love." After six months of communicating long distance, C decided to move to France to live with D. She was just twenty at the time. The first six months were blissful, C explained, but then slowly and insidiously D had become abusive. In the beginning, he had been very controlling and possessive; he hadn't "allowed" C any time with the few friends she had made in France. He had told her how to dress, because he believed women in relationships shouldn't wear such sexy clothes. When she defied any of his "rules," he devalued her and compromised her self-worth, and as time went on, he began to hit her.

C further described the abuse becoming progressively worse over time. D blamed C for all their problems, and eventually C also began to believe that she was solely responsible. "It's entirely my fault. Everything that has happened is my fault," she sobbed, which indicated to me that C still felt responsible for D's need to control her and physically hurt her. Emotional abuse can be equally or more damaging to its victims than physical abuse, because it can be so subtly destructive that it is often difficult for victims to identify. By the time the victims realize that they are being emotionally abused, their self-esteem is so damaged that they have difficulty recognizing that they are not at fault. I believe that this is what had happened to C.

C described one experience where D, in a fit of rage, had "accidently" tripped her, breaking her leg. On numerous occasions, C whispered, "He forced me to have sex. I think he raped me." I painfully listened to her recollections of the abusive incidents, and C cried through most of the session. After six months of abuse, which culminated in C's broken leg, she had decided to leave. She had been in France for about one year. C was heartbroken, and unsure about her decision to leave D and France, but her parents insisted that she return home after hearing about her broken leg. She did.

When I tried to end our session, C continued to talk. It was clearly very difficult for her to leave. After we had overrun our allotted time by ten minutes, I finally stood up, indicating with my body language that our session was over. C slowly gathered her belongings together while continuing to talk. I tried to contain her and make reassuring statements, but still, she was not leaving. I felt overwhelmed and actually started to feel angry; I imagined physically removing her from my office. I was very uncomfortable with the way I felt. "This poor woman is pouring her heart out to me, and I am angry with her," I thought. It wasn't until a few months later that I understood why I had become so angry: from our first session together, C had felt entitled. *She* had been angry that she did not have control of the session's end.

C arrived to our next session five minutes late. I asked her how she had felt after our first session, and she stated, "It felt good to talk about it." She then continued her story. Following her departure from France, C and D continued to communicate on the telephone and online, using a webcam to see each other. D was quite angry that C had left, and denied abusing her. However, as their communications continued, D became increasingly emotionally abusive. I felt some space now for questions, and inquired, "Why do you think you have continued to participate in a relationship with D after how much he hurt you?" C started weeping. "I love him, and we were going to get married. It is my fault for leaving. I still want to be with him," she stammered. I was stunned, and I am not sure why. The dynamic that C described is very common, I wrote a doctoral dissertation about violence in intimate relationships, and I had worked clinically with a number of patients who had been abused. Yet to this day, when abused patients describe their persisting "love" for their abusers, a part of me recoils in amazement.

C further shared that approximately one year after her return home, D had married another woman and hadn't told C. At this time, he was still telling C that he wanted to marry her, but when he disappeared for a month, C had called his mother, who had informed C that D had recently been married. C described feeling devastated, betrayed, and used. How could she ever trust him again? At this point, she began to ask me endless questions a complex and frustrating dynamic that would infiltrate our relationship for many years, and eventually became a major theme throughout our therapy. C's questions revolved around two major topics. The first involved C's wanting to know whether I thought particular events were her fault, and whether I believed that if she had done something differently the outcome might have been more favorable. The second required me to explain to her why men in general, with D as her primary exemplar, behaved the way they did.

When I tried to deflect these questions and encourage her to work with me collaboratively to understand what was happening, C became angry and frustrated. She would state, "I want to know your opinion as a psychologist. That is what I am paying you for." The more I encouraged her to examine her own feelings, thoughts, and desires, instead of analyzing D's intentions, the more resistant she became. "This is *not* easy," I thought.

In order to find the patient we must look for him within ourselves.

—C. Bollas

Because C's ruminations filled our sessions, I also had difficulty gathering a history. She resisted my attempts to inquire about her or to discover her early experiences, who she was, or how she had developed emotionally. Her frantic, frenzied search for answers regarding D's behavior was all she could focus on at this time. Through her remarks, but never in direct answer to my inquiries, I did eventually learn that C was twenty-five-years old, lived alone in Brooklyn, and worked as a broker. I also learned that C was from a first-generation Polish family; she and her parents had come to New York when C was four. C recalled continuous fighting in her home growing up, particularly surrounding financial stressors. She also described serving as the intermediary between her parents and their new environment during her childhood (she became *parentified*), because her parents did not speak English and did not assimilate with American culture. C recalled her childhood as lonely and sad. When I imagined C's home growing up, I saw and felt darkness all around her, and imagined a house without lights.

C continued to ruminate about D for the first two years of treatment. After she had obsessively attempted to contact D for a month following his disappearance and marriage, he finally had sent her an e-mail. He apologized for not telling her that he had gotten married, but he blamed C by indicating that he had had no choice but to marry someone else once she had left France. C, anxious and frenzied, asked, "Is this true? Could it be my fault?" I encouraged her to answer her own question. After attempting emphatically to persuade me to answer her question for at least five minutes, she finally replied, "It is my fault." I was so tempted to say, "No, it absolutely isn't," but I held back with great effort, feeling that C was pulling me into an enactment.

D told C that he really wanted to be with her, not with his current wife, and he continued to engage with C throughout his marriage, which lasted only one year. Once his marriage ended, D continually tried to entice C to return to France by reminding her of the idyllic first six months of their relationship. C felt confused; she wanted to go, but D had violated her trust, and she no longer knew what to believe. I could hear how tortured she felt and how she agonized over her decision.

Fearful that D might start a new relationship with another woman, C finally decided to go to France for a week. Still angst-ridden while on the airplane to France, C tried to maintain the fantasy that D was her "soul-mate" and that they were meant to be together. I began to notice that C's ideas about love and commitment were overly idealized and romanticized she sometimes sounded to me as if she were reading a Harlequin novel aloud rather than recounting events in actual life. C believed that because she and D were soul mates, all that was important was that they be together, and the thoughts surrounding the abuse were inconsequential "love conquers all." This persistent fantasy would make it extremely difficult for C to experience D simply as a person with flaws, and would simultaneously protect her from having to go through a painful separation.

The shadow of Aphrodite is not always an easy one to see. A sexual attraction may at first seem innocent and light, and a new romance may be filled with positive images of the other person and of the future. Yet we all know that both sex and romance can lead into difficult relationships that are suffered and endured for years, and that sex can lead to parenthood or abortion, to sexually transmitted disease, or, utterly dark, to abusive and even murderous relationships.

—Thomas Moore, *Soul Mates*

C returned from her trip to France filled with despair and uncertainty. D either had ignored her or treated her poorly during the entire trip. He would run off with his friends without inviting C, leave her alone in her hotel room, and say he was busy. When he did spend time with her, he was diminishing and devaluing. He did not even offer to drive C to the airport. C felt very confused about why D had even asked her to come to France, and when she confronted him about his behavior, he denied that he was doing anything hurtful. Upon her return to therapy, C again began her incessant and desperate questioning. If she had done *this*, would he have acted differently? If she had done *that*, would he have acted differently? I felt frustrated and backed against a wall. Her turmoil was overpowering, and I did not think answering her questions would be therapeutically helpful, but she was relentless.

I wondered with C what she expected of me; what would my answering these questions do for her? She explained that she was so bewildered, she did not understand his behavior, and she *needed to know*! Her intensity in these moments was all—encompassing, and filled the room to such a degree that I often felt suffocated. I continued to try to redirect her back to her own experience and away from her ruminations about D and his motivations.

One session was so intense that I finally told her that in my professional opinion, my answering her questions would not be helpful to her. Then, though it was premature in our therapy to do so, I further explained that sometimes, when we don't understand why something has happened, or when what has happened feels out of our control, we blame ourselves. We do this, I added, to give ourselves a semblance of control over our circumstances, which, I explained, is better than feeling helpless, and I sensed that this is how she felt helpless. C admitted, "Yes, I feel helpless, but what happened? I need to know!" "Oy," I thought. I was *so* frustrated by the magnitude and form of her resistance.

I needed to take a step back; I could tell by C's effect on me that I was engaged in an enactment. If I was going to help her, I needed to understand what she was communicating by the way she was relating to me; I had to think about the relational process between us. At this time, C began to call me frequently, outside of the session hour. At first, she called at least four times a week, and sometimes as many as four or five times in one day. Often, the messages she left in my voice mail were marked as "urgent." These calls all contained frenzied questions about her day-to-day exchanges with D. One holiday weekend, C called many times, and described feeling so distressed that she didn't know how she was going to make it through. I told her that I might need to call 911 and hospitalize her (though I wasn't genuinely worried about her safety, because I knew that these calls were aggressive and part of an enactment). As I suspected, "No, I'm fine," she demurred, and I didn't hear from her again for the remainder of the weekend. We hung up, and as I sat outside of Starbuck's with a backache, it hit me like a ton of bricks: C and I were engaged in a sadomasochistic relationship. The intrusive phone calls were aggressive. Our relational dynamic paralleled the relationship between C and D. I was relieved to have realized this, but my back continued to feel tight for the rest of the weekend.

C arrived at our following session and anxiously began discussing the status of her recent exchanges with D. Basically, since her trip to France, she and D had been primarily communicating via the Internet, with an occasional phone call. He would beguile her by stating that he still wanted to marry her, and mentioning that he planned to visit her in New York. C would believe him, and then he would disappear for days or weeks at a time, leaving C hopelessly fantasizing about where he was and what he might be doing. She always blamed herself for his indifference and for his refusal to respond to her endless messages. Sometimes, C explained, she would send him as many as five or six instant messages or e-mails a day, and still she would receive no response.

"Here is my opening," I thought. I asked C about her phone calls to me. I wondered with her if she had a sense of what she felt while calling three to four times in succession without even giving me the chance to call her back.

Surprisingly, C remarked that she felt very angry. She described thinking, "Where is she? Why isn't she calling me back? Why is she avoiding me?" She remarked that she experienced my lack of response as a purposeful avoidance (though I often had no chance to respond the phone calls were sometimes only ten minutes apart), and that this left her feeling abandoned, crazed, and furious. She would then continue to call until I picked up.

I validated C's experience. I then created curiosity by exploring with her the possibility that I had been unable to return her calls immediately. We discussed alternative reasons why I might have been inaccessible. "I guess you could be with other patients, or busy with your family. Maybe you didn't receive the message right away," she timidly remarked. We explored how her experience with me mirrored her feelings about D. She was relatively resistant to expressing any anger toward D, and instead blamed herself for his lack of response, directing the aggression she felt inward, towards herself.

As we continued treatment, my interventions with C were careful and complex, especially as they related to D. C met my encouragement to open up the therapeutic space and create curiosity surrounding her anger towards D with resistance and further self-blame. Then C would begin her customary series of questions. "So it is my fault," C would often conclude, distorting what I had said. I hypothesized that if C were to acknowledge how truly angry she was at D, she would have to separate from him. At this point in treatment, it was clear through her rigid and inflexible defenses that she was not ready for this. Instead, I was angry with D for her, which added to the complexity of our co-created relational dynamics.

We were in the middle of our second year of treatment together, and the phone calls had significantly diminished. They would still occur when C was in her crisis mode, but they had tapered to about two times a week, and C had also become able to wait for me to return her calls. However, a new frustrating dynamic had begun. C had developed the habit of arriving to our sessions about ten minutes late. She would then inevitably have difficulty leaving or, more accurately, she would refuse to leave when our allotted time had expired. Over time, this pattern became more pronounced. Now C would constantly arrive fifteen to twenty minutes late for session with an excuse, and would violate the therapeutic frame by not respecting the boundary of the session's end. This enraged me. As I distanced myself from the dynamic once again, I was able to formulate that C was unconsciously inducing my rage. Again, C felt angry with me for setting boundaries and limits on our time together. To her, these boundaries felt like rejection, abandonment, and dismissal. C was unable to process these feelings, yet communicated them through her actions, and I, as a container for her split-off affect, experienced them instead. This was valuable information, but painful, uncomfortable, and frustrating.

The therapist's role is not just to allow her emotional disturbance to be within the safer setting of the therapeutic relationship. Within this setting, these feelings can be reflected on and learned from. The therapist provides a container that holds, tames, metabolizes, and detoxifies feelings that would otherwise be too unsettling for the patient to tolerate.

—Howard E. Book

C began to relate extraordinarily alarming exchanges with D. After disappearing for some time, he would eventually reconnect, using some distorted rationale to convince C that she had been responsible for his absence. He often named something C had done or said that had injured him, and he claimed that he had needed time "to get over it." This reinforced C's worst fear, that everything *was* her fault. The exchanges became increasingly disturbing. D would demand that C remove her clothing in front of the webcam so that he could see her. Afraid that he would dismiss her again, C would indulge him despite feeling uncomfortable. On numerous occasions, C would disrobe for D, who would continue communication for approximately one week before disappearing again, which left C distraught, confused, and humiliated. Again, C started relentlessly questioning whether she had done something wrong. However, now she had also begun to question whether she was "lowering herself," or giving up her dignity. Still, she continued to engage with D.

I was curious with her why she persisted in her communication. C still held on to her idealized vision of the first six months of their relationship. She did not understand where this original D, who had been so attentive and loving, had gone. She had fantasies that eventually that person would show himself again, and that they could be married. "Yeah, yeah. And then you can live 'happily ever after'," I thought, exhausted. How was I to respect C's need to cling to this ideal image of D, while slowly breaking down her resistance and helping her to see how clearly disturbed and abusive he was?

Illusion is a dangerous condition, and yet we continue to place naïve trust in this kind of love, and we enjoy movies and novels that depict these illusions. Critics complain about the unrealistic way in which love is portrayed in romantic stories, but audiences and readers continue to watch these movies and read these books avidly. In our childish attachment to romance, we are championing the way of the soul its thirst for pleasure, and its inescapable need for experiences that may or may not be conducive to productive lives.

—Thomas Moore, *Soul Mates*

I truly liked C. I found her defensive structure to be one of the most frustrating I had encountered in my entire career, but beneath this I could feel the essence of her humanity. C was kind, genuine, thoughtful, interesting, and very generous. I was saddened when I thought about how her underlying way of relating with others was destroying her. Despite my frustrations, I really wanted to help her.

We were in our third year of treatment together, and C was still engaging with D, although the extent of their communication had significantly diminished. D was initiating contact less and less, and C and I were working hard to help her sit with her feelings of anxiety. C had finally become able to cease making the first move to contact D, although it was causing her immense grief. When D did contact her, it was often to ask to see her naked via the webcam. Finally, C was able to say no. She felt that exposing herself to him after he had acted so poorly would be relinquishing her dignity; maintaining her self-respect was very important to her now. Despite her progress, she continued with her questions. I began to feel that she needed reassurance that these humiliating and degrading demands were not her fault. Strikingly, I also had begun to feel that now, on some level, she actually knew that she wasn't to blame. Yet she continued to engage with D.

C came into session one afternoon absolutely unraveled. D had contacted her the previous evening for the first time in over a month. Via the webcam, he had asked C to remove her clothing for him. When C refused, he became aggressive and began to pressure C, threatening to send previous nude photos of her to her parents and to her office. C was completely beside herself, and terrified that D would follow through with his threat. She sobbed. In addition to feeling betrayed by his menacing comments, remarkably, she still wondered whether they might have been together if she had done something differently. D, naturally, had alluded to this possibility. While threatening her, he had also simultaneously attempted to entice her to disrobe by promising that he would come visit her. C was terribly confused. "Did he really mean it? Should I have done what he wanted?"

I was beside myself with fury towards D, but also towards C. Her need to cling to her self-immolating, idyllic fantasies left me fuming. "How can she not acknowledge his abusiveness?!" I raged to myself. Rationally, I knew that such denial was her defense mechanism, but I could feel myself on the verge of losing control, which is the antithesis of my usual demeanor. As C continued to wonder whether D really wanted to be with her, I finally lost control. "He *doesn't* want to be with you! A man who loves you and wants to spend his life with you does *not* behave like this!" I stated powerfully, raising my voice. I was horrified by my loss of control. This was not a planned psychotherapy technique it was me, a seasoned therapist, responding emotionally because I was ensconced in an enactment.

C never responded to D again. The technique worked, even though it was ill-informed. When I explored C's feelings surrounding my intervention, she actually thanked me, stating, "I am glad you were so straightforward." This is not usually the way I work, but I made a mental note of this potent interaction and wondered if I needed to modify my technique a bit in order to help C. D still contacted her intermittently. She never responded, but she did still torture herself with thoughts surrounding what she might have done differently. She continued to take responsibility for the demise of the relationship, and she continued her interminable questioning. I began to reiterate that I believed her self-blame was a symptom of her need to manufacture a sense of control over a situation that made her feel helpless. Feeling responsible, and believing that her questions had definitive answers (if only she could figure them out), was far easier and less painful than to feel powerless. Such a dynamic is quite common in people who have experienced trauma. C heard what I said, I think, but her tormenting self-blame continued. I began to understand this as fundamental to C's personality organization self-blame was a deeply embedded lens through which C experienced herself and her world. Such ingrained structures of subjective reality are very difficult to adjust, because they are elemental to each individual's experience of Heidegger's "being-in-the-world."

At the beginning of our fourth year of treatment, C met a new man, B. For the first time, she was excited and even cheerful; I had never before had the pleasure of experiencing C smile. She began to discuss the details of their first two dates. B was warm, his cultural background was similar to C's, and she felt instantly connected to him. She was a bit anxious, which seemed appropriate for the beginning stages of a relationship. B took C out to an expensive restaurant for their first date; on the second date, he bought her flowers. This "ideal" romance lasted for approximately one month, when

B started to pull back. He provided no genuine explanation he would say simply that he was busy, or tired, or simply unavailable. This behavior was toxic for C. She began to call me outside of session again not as frequently as when she had been at her worst, but more frequently than during the previous year. C was beside herself, and again wanted to know what had happened. Of course, C blamed herself, although she couldn't figure out what she had done.

Remembering the success of my earlier "straightforward" intervention, I asked C if it was difficult to imagine that B simply wasn't interested. She responded, "But *why*? We had such a strong connection. Do you think it is because I didn't sleep with him?" "Here we go again," I thought, already exhausted and frustrated. C continued to call B, attempting to make plans with him. He would talk for hours with her on the phone, but never followed through with any of their plans. Eventually, C felt as though she were relinquishing her dignity by pursuing B, and she stopped calling him however, she continued to create romanticized fantasies about "what might have been."

I began to address her phone calls to me. She would call at any hour, from 7am to midnight. When she needed to call, she had no boundaries. We discussed increasing our sessions to twice a week, as once a week clearly wasn't containing her. C responded that she couldn't afford it. I learned through this discussion that C's father accessed and monitored her bank account. C was twenty-eight years old by now. Her parents didn't know she was in therapy, and she wouldn't be able to explain the absence of so much money to her father if she had to pay for two sessions each week. Try as I might, C provided no further background information, but I thought this disclosure was interesting. Our compromise was that she would have her usual session once each week, with the addition of one paid fifteen-minute phone call between sessions. Having established appropriate boundaries, this arrangement worked well.

C's mood was now quite dysphoric, and she was angry; she pointedly repeated that things never work out for her. Her mood colored all her thought processes. I felt such darkness in the room with her when I would think about our sessions, I imagined our sitting in my office with the lights out. This paralleled my images of her childhood home. I tried a new approach. I shared with C how lovely I found her to be. She was gentle, warm, giving, and thoughtful. She was beautiful, with long, silky, dark brown hair, penetrating dark brown eyes, and a trim, curvy body. She smiled and softly thanked me. I believe she took in what I had shared. I also sensed that my having disclosed my thoughts about her had soothed her. I felt an intimacy growing between us after that session; she was more aware of me in the room, and managed to adhere more diligently to the therapeutic boundaries.

A mood assails us. It comes from neither from "outside" nor from "inside," but arises out of Being-in-the-world, as a way of such Being.

—Martin Heidegger,
Being and Time

In the middle of our fifth year of therapy, C was becoming involved with a new man, N. At first, they were friends, but slowly their feelings became romantic. Their relationship evolved slowly, but was appropriate, and N made himself very available to C. He was kind and thoughtful, was supportive of C, and made it clear that he liked her very much. For the first few months, before the relationship became serious, C was joyful and contented. However, as their relationship progressed, C began to bring up her fears of committing fully to N. C thought about B he fit her idealized image of with whom she should be, while N didn't. Despite how fabulously they got along, how much fun they had together, and how secure N clearly made C feel, he did not measure up to her idealized image of her "soul mate."

We spent months exploring the paradoxical nature of C's desires. She wanted to be with a man who treated her well and made her feel the way N did. Yet she clung to fantasies of a man she barely knew. I opened up the therapeutic space by encouraging C to explore possible reasons she held on to B. She described what she had experienced as the intensity of their connection, and revealed that she didn't feel as passionately towards N. She also found it difficult to let go of thoughts of B because she never knew why he had lost interest. C painfully contemplated, over numerous sessions, whether she should contact B and ask him what had happened. They were now friends on Facebook, and had exchanged a few harmless e-mails during the past year. Should she contact him or not? C wanted my answer. I encouraged her to explore the reality of their relatively brief romantic encounter. C understood, but her fantasies about who B essentially was, and what it would be like to be with him, overpowered her rational thinking.

Romantic love is an illusion.

—Thomas Moore, *Soul Mates*

It was quite difficult to sit with C's idealizations of romantic love, and I was fearful that she would jeopardize her current relationship. C was aware of this risk. She had grown to love N, and didn't want to hurt him or destroy the relationship. She was able to resist her desire to contact B, but her intermittent thoughts about doing so remained.

C is still in treatment with me. We are beginning our seventh year together. Her boundaries are more appropriate, and when she does attempt to cross a boundary, she quickly recognizes it. She is still seeing N, and their relationship has become quite serious. She still thinks about contacting B, but has been able to contain this impulse. We are working collaboratively to better understand her difficulty in feeling contented, and to fill the room with a lightness that she has never been quite able to embrace.

Chapter 4

"Mirror, Mirror on the Wall: Am I Pretty (Do I Exist at All)?"

You need not, and in fact cannot, teach an acorn to grow into an oak tree, but when given a chance, its intrinsic potentialities will develop.

—Karen Horney, *Neurosis and Human Growth*

The first thing I noticed about T when she came in for our first session was her striking beauty. Dressed casually in jeans and a T-shirt, she had silky, perfectly straight, long dark hair, olive skin, high cheekbones, and pearl-shaped turquoise eyes. She stood tall and seemed confident with her 5'10" stature, and appeared as if she just walked off the cover of a magazine.

I didn't know much about why T had decided to come in for psychotherapy, other than that her primary care physician had referred her for chronic stomach pain that had no known organic origin. As what became a twice-weekly course of treatment over eight years began, I learned that T's outward appearance was incongruent with her inner world, which was a private place filled with self-hatred, worthlessness, and a constant struggle to figure out who she really was.

At the beginning of treatment, T focused on her chronic stomach pain, coupled with the fear that she would lose control of her bowels. This pain and fear had resulted in T's leaving her occupation as a teacher, for fear that she would lose control while in front of her students. It was difficult for T to experience her symptoms as psychological, despite the numerous tests that suggested there was no known medical explanation. She adamantly clung to the notion that her ailment was physical, and we began her treatment by focusing on her frustrations surrounding the fact that the numerous tests she had taken and the many doctors she had seen could not explain the cause. I joined T in her frustrations in the beginning, despite my intuitive sense that her symptoms were likely psychological in origin, and were a sort of somatic communication of what was buried beneath.

As the treatment and our relationship unfolded, I learned that T was twenty-nine years old, and had grown up in a household in which external appearance was of primary importance. No emphasis or attention fostered inner human growth potential, and no importance was placed on unique interests, strengths, or inner development. All that mattered in T's house was that she looked the way her parents thought she should. T's mother had undergone multiple plastic surgeries, as had T, I would later find out. T described the necessity of having perfectly rounded, pushed-up C-cup breasts, a small rounded nose, flawless skin, and a flat stomach in order to be loved and admired by her parents.

T described her numerous plastic surgeries, which began at the age of nine when she and her mother underwent simultaneous rhinoplasties. Following that, T had two breast surgeries and three liposuctions on her stomach area. Still unsatisfied with what she perceived as flab around her stomach area, T planned more liposuction and possibly lip enhancement. T's descriptions of her surgeries were noticeably mechanical; I sensed that T completely lacked a connection with her body. To her, her body was an object that could be, and "should" be, manipulated, until she felt it was perfect.

In exploring the connection between these surgeries, her presenting symptoms, and a childhood that required her to be a paragon of physical beauty, T was very resistant to experiencing or verbalizing any psychic distress aside from a pervasive dissatisfaction with her appearance. T believed that she needed these surgeries, and only these surgeries, to feel better, and that no amount of psychological exploration would help her. Yet, she continued to come to our sessions, which indicated to me that she did have some insight that her symptoms, particularly her feelings about her self-image, contained some psychological meaning.

As T's clinician, my goal was to create enough psychological curiosity in her that she might begin to question ways that her symptoms reflected deep-rooted and painful feelings surrounding her sense of self. Working collaboratively, which I believe is vitally important for a positive therapeutic outcome, we slowly began to understand T's stomach as a place where she contained her anxiety, and to view her chronic pains as expressions of disquiet. T slowly began to be open to this interpretation, which in turn opened up the therapeutic space for psychological exploration of her self-hatred, feelings of worthlessness, and impoverished inner world.

As therapy progressed, it became increasingly clear that T was completely alienated from her inner thoughts and desires, particularly her inner strengths, and that therefore, she vehemently needed to retain an emphasis on her physicality. The idea that releasing this emphasis on her physical being would require her to separate from long-standing ideals and identity formations that had been set forth by her parents from the time she was a child complicated therapy. T described her childhood home as decorated with artwork depicting idealized female bodies with supple breasts, perfectly small noses, small waists, and flat stomachs. T felt she fell short of this ideal, and believed that plastic surgery was the only way to meet it, until she began to question this supposition in therapy.

Each session with T began with my re-experiencing her striking beauty and her seemingly confident cadence and manner. As time went on, the incongruity between her presentation and the smoldering self-hatred she experienced internally became clearer and clearer. She also reported such incongruity in her outside life. For example, she often received compliments about her appearance, which felt very paradoxical to her inner experience of herself. Her discussion of these experiences provided an opening for us to explore the connection between the unrealistic nature of the ideals that were presented to her in childhood and her own ideals of beauty, particularly her own.

In addition to the challenges now presented by T's vacillation between identifying her underlying self-hatred and returning to her primary defense of focusing on her dissatisfaction with her physical self, T began to reveal that she often engaged in destructive intimate relationships. She described instances in which she would sleep with men in order to feel desirable and attractive, only to be left feeling more empty and worthless. Despite her insight about the destructiveness of this behavior, T described feeling unable to stop herself. At moments, her primary need to feel desired externally became all encompassing, and she would engage in sex impulsively.

In collaboration, T and I began to connect her feelings of worthlessness as well as the alienation of her desire to be in a healthy, intimate relationship to her tendency to respond impulsively when experiencing self-hatred. In response to our many sessions exploring this topic, T began to get involved with a man who truly cared about her, and who was interested in a relationship. T spent many sessions exploring her ambivalence, as well as her fear of becoming intimate with someone who would eventually see beneath her "mask." We also explored what it was like for her to be with someone who accepted her for who she was, and who didn't have idealized expectations. T's uncertainty about her fundamental identity aside from her physical traits compounded our process.

In establishing uniqueness in the therapeutic relationship, T and I explored her inner potentials, and she slowly began to uncover and integrate the strengths, desires, and interests that constructed her inner world. T had never explored any of the inner desires or strengths that defined her as a unique and special person. Instead, she had always been *viewed*, through the objectifying gaze of others, as an external shell that could never live up to physical expectations. She was left feeling empty, worthless, and lost in terms of self-identity. Through our new emphasis on inner strivings, T became more aware and able to embrace her uniqueness as a whole person.

As the treatment progressed, T's stomach pains began to dissipate. She began a graduate program in physical therapy, but continued to discuss her desire to undergo more liposuction. In addition, T began to describe uncomfortable sweating around her groin and upper thigh area, and was seeking a doctor who would remove the sweat glands from this area. This symptom became so pronounced that at the beginning of one session, T was so uncomfortable sitting on the leather chair in my office that she believed she would leave sweat marks that I would see. Although I tried to process this as clinical material, T's discomfort made her so ill at ease that I had to replace her chair with a canvas one, borrowed from an adjoining office.

T and I spent months discussing ways that these symptoms might relate to the atmosphere in which she grew up that her feelings about her body might in fact communicate discomfort with her inner being, and allow her to avoid underlying painful feelings relating to her identity and sense of self by diverting her focus outward. T did have cognitive insight at this time. That is, she understood, on an intellectual level, what her symptoms meant. Emotionally, however, T remained attached to her early identity development organization, and as a result, despite our hours of discussion in session, she went on to have her fourth liposuction surgery.

I felt that I had failed T as a clinician. Despite our years of work together, she still was unable to integrate her own beliefs and desires, or separate from the ideas imposed on her as a child. However, when T returned following her surgery, she revealed shame and dissonance that she had gone through with the procedure. She felt she had given in. She even began to express rage toward her parents, which indicates major progress for a patient with such symptomology. Her rage was significant because it reflected T's growing ability to separate from her parental ideals. These ideals, until now, had been the primary organizing features of her identity.

During this time, T was also becoming more involved and intimate in her romantic relationship. This man, R, was a healthy and stable person, who seemed emotionally able to hold and tolerate T's vacillations between pushing him away and pulling him close, a pattern quite common among individuals struggling with identity formation. T frequently described her fears about being emotionally exposed as not having her "mask" to protect her. Metaphorically, T's label of the "mask" was very creative: it described her psychological defenses, and illustrated the protective mechanisms related to her physicality.

Using the therapeutic dyad as a microcosm of other outside relationships, we were able to discuss T's relatedness and openness in sessions. When T began treatment, her ruminations and fixation on her physical self had kept her from having to relate to me in a truly engaged manner. As she began to establish a more secure identity, her comportment in sessions became more genuinely engaged and connected. We explored what this experience was like for her, and we discussed what it was like for her to gradually drop her "mask." T was able to connect her feeling that I embraced her inner unique qualities to a gradual feeling of safety, which prefaced a profound development in her ability to let go of her "mask" in sessions.

Following these sessions, T came into therapy one afternoon and announced that she was moving in with R. She continued to discuss her fears, but was able to process and clearly articulate her desire to be with R and take this next step of commitment. During this time, T also spent many sessions describing anger towards her parents, and revealed that she had begun to communicate her feelings to them. T's feelings were often met with retaliatory anger and resistance, particularly from her mother, but she was strong enough now to persist in her convictions. It was through this ability to separate from the ideals imposed by her parents that T was able to make, recognize, and own her decision to be with R, a decision that made her happy. T, once unable to understand or take ownership of any of her desires, was finally able to distinguish what she wanted for herself.

T still discussed discomfort with her body, particularly what she experienced as her soft stomach, but she was also able to recognize that this uneasiness was a direct result of her parents' preoccupation with physical perfection. She no longer discussed the desire to have plastic surgery, but rather was able to sit with her feelings and verbalize them both to R and in therapy. She also began to understand her experience of sweating as a somatic expression of the toxic self-hatred oozing out of her. As she became increasingly able to find words for her bodily sensations, this symptom dissipated.

Maynard Gull, you have the freedom to be yourself, your true self, here and now, and nothing can stand in your way.

—Richard Bach, *Jonathan Livingston Seagull*

Just as an acorn inherently develops into an oak tree, given the nurturing atmosphere of therapy, T began to grow into her real self: a strong, ambitious woman, capable of attaining her goals. By this time, T had almost completed her graduate program, and she was preparing to take her board examinations. She did suffer from moderate and appropriate anxiety surrounding this endeavor, but felt a new sense of confidence and control. This was foreign to her historical out-of-control experiences in the face of challenges, but at this time, T knew she could conquer the exams. T did indeed pass her boards, and with a score so high, she was nearly first in her class.

T's next objective was to start her own private physical therapy practice, a goal that R supported and even helped her with financially. T was very disappointed that she did not receive the same support or acknowledgment from her parents, but she tried to maintain a healthy perspective about her parents' limitations. Her mother was preparing to have her third breast surgery just as T was starting her practice, and we spent many sessions discussing T's rage toward her mother's constant preoccupation with herself and her appearance.

T also began to express rage in relation to how her mother dressed. "A woman in her sixties with her cleavage constantly exposed a complete lack of class," T revealed. This was the first time T had described her mother's appearance with disgust; until now, her descriptions had been filled with envy. Again, this was a significant indication that T was separating from the imposing, noxious, and once-internalized parental ideals from which her symptoms originated. At times, T would share fantasies about having more surgeries. These fantasies seemed always to be triggered by injurious comments T's mother would make about T's appearance. At this point in T's development, her inner world and her sense of self were developed enough that she knew she would not undergo surgery, but her mother's disapproval left her feeling dysphoric and lonely. T was appropriately saddened that she would never have the relationship with her mother that she wanted a relationship in which she was admired, appreciated, and loved for her special and unique self, rather than a relationship in which she was criticized for the color of her lipstick.

T began to discuss her "mask" again, but this time it was both symbolic and literal. T had a family wedding to attend. Traditionally, for formal events such as this, T's mother, her mother's sisters, and T would have their hair and makeup done professionally. T, now aware of her true self, what she truly wanted, and how she preferred to appear, did not want to participate in this family tradition. T felt that the makeup, in particular, was a "mask," and she was able to recognize that she did not like wearing "all that makeup." Incidentally, having sat across from T for many years, I could not even imagine what she might look like with a lot of makeup, she was so naturally beautiful. We spent many sessions exploring T's conflict surrounding whether she should join her family, or take ownership of her own desire and do what made her comfortable. T wanted to act in congruence with her inner self, but this required another step toward separation. Psychologically, if T let down her "mask," she would also expose her true self to her entire family. Without the safe hiding place her "mask" provided, T felt everyone would see who she really was, and this terrified her.

T's mother was very resistant to T's tentative decision not to partake in the family tradition. This enraged T, but simultaneously compromised her ability to remain true to how she felt. T still longed for her mother's approval and acceptance, but she also was struggling to use her newfound inner resources. She had become proud of who she was, but she was still rightfully afraid of enduring injuries to this pride from her family. It was a painful and telling conflict for T, as she began to see her mother as envious of her ability to remain true to herself despite the possible perceptions of others. We spent many sessions discussing T's painful conflict surrounding her decision-making in the weeks leading up to the wedding.

As T left our session just prior to the wedding, it was not even clear to me what her decision would be. The potency of her conflict filled the room as she departed still struggling, conflicted, and undecided. It wasn't until I received a voice mail message from T late Saturday afternoon, in which she declared that she was "going without [her] mask," that I learned her decision. This turning point occurred towards the end of our seventh year of work together, and I glowed with satisfaction and was filled with emotion as I listened to T's message. Prior to this, T had made tremendous strides towards finding her inner strengths, recognizing what her bodily symptoms communicated, and establishing an integrated self. Being able to make the courageous decision to separate from her parents' ideals and traditions enough to expose herself reflected an accumulation of all the accomplishments we had achieved in therapy.

T came into our next session with stories that illustrated her family's responses (particularly her mother's) to her attending the wedding without her "mask." To T's surprise, many of her relatives commented on how beautiful she looked. Unfortunately, T's mother did not respond so positively. Her mother continually commented on T's understated appearance, and even went to the extreme of humiliating T by pointing out what she perceived as T's flaws to T's family and friends. T was filled with an appropriate mix of rage and sadness. T then described her attempts to get her mother to acknowledge and appreciate her, but she was continually disappointed.

In the last year that T and I worked together, we spent many of our sessions focused on T's learning to accept her mother's limitations and finding ways to maintain a somewhat comfortable relationship with her. We also worked on her possible impending engagement to R and the establishment of her physical therapy practice. At this point, T had integrated her thoughts, strengths, and desires, and was able to make decisions that felt harmonious with her inner being.

T still expressed rage towards her mother for not providing a nurturing environment or cultivating her inner strengths, but she began to find some comfort in her ability to maintain a secure sense of self in the face of her mother's critical nature. T also was able to experience herself as a special and worthy person who deserved a stable, loving, and secure relationship. T and R became engaged, and were married just prior to our termination of treatment. T and I discussed the termination of her treatment for three months prior to its ending. T felt that she had gained the resources she needed to continue her growth and development on her own. I wasn't so sure, but I had to respect her desire to terminate therapy. She did understand that she could return to therapy at any time if she felt it was necessary. As I watched T leave our last session, I felt sad; there was much more I felt she needed to work on. I wondered and hoped that she would be able to remain true to herself and to her marriage.

Chapter 5

"I Used to Love Bread"

The experience of hunger is not only rooted in the body, but also develops through experiences with others.

—Janet Tintner, *Bypassing barriers to change?*
Bariatric surgery, case material

I was in my office one afternoon, eating lunch and enjoying some rare leisure time between appointments, when my phone rang. "Hmm, an unfamiliar number. Should I pick it up?" I wondered. I usually don't, but on that day, I did. The woman's voice on the other end sounded frantic; at first, it was difficult even to decipher what she was saying. I tried to calm her down enough so that her speech would be coherent. Finally, with great effort, I learned that I was speaking with Mrs. W, and that she was calling on behalf of her nineteen-year-old daughter, who, Mrs. W anxiously shared, "wouldn't eat." The conversation lasted at least fifteen minutes, maybe more, and felt eternal. Mrs. W was so concerned and distraught about her daughter's condition that I could not get her off the phone. Eventually, I was able to set up an appointment with her daughter, L, for the following Monday, and I offered Mrs. W a referral so that she might see her own psychologist for help with her obvious anxiety surrounding her daughter's "condition." She graciously declined, and we hung up. I was exhausted. I wondered why L had not called to make her own appointment. I felt that her mother's calling in her stead communicated something significant, and I was sure I would find out the meaning soon enough.

L came to our session the following Monday. After the usual initial introductions, she immediately began discussing what she considered her restrictive eating. She would eat one egg white in the morning, two slices of half-calorie bread with one slice of fat-free turkey for lunch, and one plain chicken breast for dinner. She would sometimes eat fat-free cookies or yogurt for dessert. We spent the entire session discussing her relationship with food. L explained that until approximately a year ago, when she had started college, she had eaten whatever she wanted. The self-restricting had begun slowly, and seemed to be getting worse. She described thinking about food all the time for example, she would spend her leisure time surfing the internet in search of new fat-free cookies to try. She resented the other girls in her dorm, whom she viewed as able to eat whatever they wanted.

I listened attentively to the progression of her restrictiveness, and I wondered with L if she had any sense of why or how she had begun to restrict. She described that she felt "fat." The fat she described was ostensibly around her stomach area. "It's genetic," she explained. It seemed to get worse when she began college, so she had decided to go on a diet; slowly, the "diet" involved eating less and less food. L knew that this was a problem, but she insisted, "I can't stop restricting, or I'll get fat." This began our five-year, once-weekly therapeutic journey together.

At the beginning of our second session, I provided L with the name of a physician who specialized in eating disorders, and made it very clear that she needed to see this doctor monthly if we were to work successfully together. At this point, I was not excessively worried about L's weight, though later, I would be. She was 5'2" and teetering around 98 pounds: petite, very thin, and in the "low-normal" range for a healthy body weight. She had lost ten pounds during the past year. She continued to menstruate, but her periods were becoming lighter, and her cycle, which used to be a reliable twenty-eight days, was now much longer.

Our early sessions focused on L's obsession with food. She endlessly described everything she ate each week, the foods she had restricted herself from eating, and her incessant search for new fat-free treats. I listened as attentively as possible, but found the sessions boring and lifeless. L was quite unrelated and disengaged at the beginning of our therapeutic process, and I knew, both intuitively and from my experiences with patients with disordered eating, that I had to find a way to create a relationship between us. From a relational perspective, disordered eating reflects a primary dysfunction in the ability to relate interpersonally. The primary relationship for patients with disordered eating is a relationship with food.

Regardless of presentation, disordered eating may be a sign that the patient is locked in a narrow, isolating world of preoccupation, obsession, and despair.

The superficiality of dieting and bodily concern may hide a severe withdrawal from intimate and interpersonal interactions.

—Jean Petrucelli, *Treating Eating Disorders*

As treatment progressed, I began to inquire about L's childhood experiences and about how her family had treated food when she was a child. L had been a gymnast for many years, and she explained that because of her participation in this sport, she had always been self-conscious of her body. As she had begun to develop, she became even more aware of her shapely but muscular physique. L's parents were overweight, and so was her five-year-older sister. They all carried their extra weight in their stomach area, and L was terrified that she would lose her flat belly. As she approached puberty, she had also begun to notice that her gymnast friends were thinner than she was. L described herself as "petite but muscular." She had always wanted to be skinny, but had never formally dieted until college. She described her secret envy of the other college girls, and the shame that had surrounded her body image since she had been about twelve years old.

L also described difficulty making and maintaining friendships. She often had been excluded from parties and other gathering of friends from school. L described feeling lonely and bored much of the time, particularly during the summer months, when she didn't have her studies on which to focus. Her primary relationship was with her mother, with whom she spent most of her time. L began to open up about the complexity of their relationship. L's mother was very anxious, overbearing, and controlling. She was excessively critical, and despite L's numerous talents, exceptional grades, and high aspirations, her mother always found reasons why L wasn't good enough. In fact, in spite of L's obvious gifts, her mother consistently used distorted rationales to argue that L was not capable of achieving her goals. She dissuaded her aspirations, and provided little or no support for L's efforts. Conversely, I experienced L as an exceptional young woman, wise beyond her years, with high aspirations and an unquestionable ability to accomplish her goals. Sitting across from L and listening to her stories, I felt enraged, though L showed little emotion (it was far too early in her treatment).

L provided a great example of her mother's astonishing lack of support. When L had decided she wanted to go away to college and live on campus, possibly even out of state, her mother had told her that she would not survive alone at school. She insisted that L live at home and commute to school, pointing out that with L's problems sustaining friendships, she would never be able to get along with a roommate. This battle between them lasted for months, until finally they reached a compromise: L would attend a university close enough to home that she could return every weekend. When I probed L for her feelings about this struggle, she remarked, "That's how my mother is. There is nothing I can do." Her affect was relatively flat as she discussed this, and I felt that L was passively acquiescing in order to preserve the integrity of what I came to understand as her overly enmeshed relationship with her mother.

L also recounted her mother's critiques of her appearance. L had grown up hearing that her sister was beautiful "the pretty one," as L's mother often said. Her sister had blonde hair and blue eyes, and was much taller than L. L believed that her sister was indeed the more beautiful sibling, and she experienced herself as unattractive. "That is why boys never show interest in me," L flatly stated. Again, sitting across from L, I was flabbergasted. She was adorable, with very dark, curly hair, porcelain skin, and bright blue eyes. When L brought some photographs to later sessions, I was even more stunned. L was just as beautiful, if not more beautiful, than her sister. L had internalized her mother's harsh statements, and believed she was unattractive, ineffectual, inadequate, and unlikable to others.

L was not only self-effacing, but also highly critical of others, which I understood to be the core of her interpersonal difficulties. The expectations she imposed on others were irrationally high, and she was consistently disappointed. She would start to develop friendships, but would eventually (and irrationally) perceive some sort of rejection and end these relationships. L needed to feel omnipotent in all areas of her life, and as soon as she perceived herself to be falling short in another's estimation, she would become angry and dysphoric. L resolved these situations by isolating herself from her peers, and spending most of her time either alone or with her harsh, critical mother.

I had not yet interpreted or intervened. I could sense L's resistance, and she could be remarkably inflexible in her thinking. She was terrified of any real relatedness, and maintained distance from me in our treatment. Though she spoke openly, and answered questions without hesitation, I could feel a profound wall between us. Her preoccupation with food, dieting, and her body was symptomatic of her fear of engaging with others. I began slowly, by encouraging her to be curious about her inner world, a place she kept deeply hidden, even from herself.

L was studying journalism in college, and she was minoring in psychology. During the spring semester of her sophomore year, she was writing a paper about *anorexia nervosa* for her psychopathology course, which opened up some space for her to be curious about what her eating symptoms might be communicating about her relationships with herself and with others. For the first time, L began to explore her ambivalent feelings towards her mother. She described feeling very close to and extremely dependent on her mother, while simultaneously wanting to be more independent and to separate a bit. However, she felt unable to disengage from her mother, and courageously began to explore why this disengagement was such an arduous process. We began collaboratively to discuss her mother's unspoken insistence upon L's remaining at home, and that L was unable to separate from her mother because of her mother's desperate need to prevent such a separation.

By her behavior, an anorexic girl tells the world: "Look, see how thin I am, even thinner than you wanted me to be. You can't make me eat more. I am in control of my fate, even if my fate is starving."

—Mary Pipher, *Reviving Ophelia: Saving the Selves of Adolescent Girls*

Over the next few months, L lost even more weight as her excessively restrictive behavior worsened. She now weighed ninety pounds, eight pounds less than her presenting weight had been. She was always cold, and she had not menstruated in three months. I became increasingly concerned about her physical well-being. At this time, L's mother would try to force L to eat. She would bake the delicious, carbohydrate-rich breads that L had once loved, and L refused. In fact, L disclosed that the more her mother pushed her, the less she ate. This, clearly, was L's way of maintaining some control over her own decisions, while firmly communicating that she had a will of her own. She used food to communicate that she was an independent person who did not have to submit to her mother's unappeasable demands.

In spite of L's growing insight and awareness, she continued to restrict her eating. She began her junior year of college emaciated, weighing only eighty-six pounds. I began to receive panic-stricken, frenzied messages from L's mother on my voice mail. At the beginning of our therapy, L and I had decided collaboratively that it would be best for L to forego signing the consent form that would allow me to speak with her mother about her condition. Her mother had commanded control over L's entire life until this point, and after some thought, we had decided that the therapeutic space was for L and L alone, and should remain free from her mother's intrusion. Though I did not return Mrs. L's calls, I did speak with L's physician.

We decided that if L were to lose any more weight, she would have to be hospitalized. I shared this with L, and she became frightened. Remarkably, for nearly one year she was able to maintain her weight at eighty-six pounds.

As treatment continued, L began to share relevant clinical material about other areas of her life. It became painfully clear that L's restrictiveness permeated her entirely, and was her stylistic and pervasive expression of Heidegger's "being-in-the-world." I listened without interpreting at this time. I feared that L might perceive any interpretive statements as criticism, and I was still working hard to help L engage genuinely with her therapy. L shared that she didn't drink, and that she in fact looked down on her peers who did. She also thought her peers' participation in any sexual experimentation was "sleazy." Her roommate was engaged in a serious romantic relationship, and when she shared with L that she had slept with her boyfriend, L was judgmental and disgusted by the thought of sexuality. Yet, L had described desperately wanting a boyfriend since we had begun our work together. When I asked her how she imagined such a relationship, she explained: "You know: holding hands, watching movies together, getting flowers, eventually kissing." I imagined a latency-age, childlike romance as L described her idealized relationship fantasies.

"Interesting," I thought. "L unconsciously would like to remain her mother's child, just as L's mother would like her to remain her child." I thought further, then, that L's food restrictions also communicated her ambivalence about separating and becoming independent from her mother: symbolically, she would be able to remain a child as long as she maintained a childlike body. L's body communicated what L could not consciously reconcile emotionally, and the origin of this conflict rested on Mrs. W's indications that she wanted and needed L to remain childlike and dependent. In addition to her covert communications, Mrs. W's criticism and undermining of L's aspirations maintained L's dependence by reinforcing her uncertainties about her own abilities and competencies. Mrs. W's overbearing and controlling way of relating to L had left L with a substantial lack of freedom and control over her own life. Cumulatively, these variables were at the origin of L's need to control her world through her restrictive eating patterns she had resolved her powerlessness in other areas of her life by excessively managing her food intake.

In order for L to establish healthy relationships with food and her body, she had to separate from her mother and begin to relate to others in a genuine and engaged manner she had to create primary relationships with people, rather than with food. I was relieved that I was now better able to conceptualize the source of L's disordered eating and lack of relatedness, and that now I had a framework from which to begin our real work together. I also knew how challenging our work was going to be.

We began our third year of treatment together, and L came into session after receiving the results of a required bone density scan. She was worried and obviously anxious; the results showed that her bones had thinned, and the doctor informed her that if she continued to restrict her diet so extremely, within a few years she would have the bones of an eighty-year-old woman. This really frightened L. She had not menstruated for over a year, and she was now trying to calculate how much weight she would have to gain in order to get her period. L was very preoccupied with her overall appearance, in conjunction with her obsessive attitude toward thinness. Hearing that damage to her bones might alter her exterior appearance terrified her.

L often spent hundreds of dollars on clothes and make-up that she clearly could not afford, and she required positive affirmations of her appearance, particularly from men, in order to maintain a veneer of self-worth. She always came to session dressed impeccably, and she spoke endlessly about shopping and clothes. She always had her makeup and hair perfectly done. It was a bit much, I thought, particularly since she was so naturally attractive.

I began to wonder how L experienced me and my appearance. Most patients notice nearly everything about their therapists. They take their therapists in, and create fantasies about us. They imagine what our lives might be like outside of the therapy room. Exploring these images and fantasies provides valuable clinical information. With a patient who presents with disordered eating, body image issues, and self-worth that is measured and modulated through the comments of others, it is virtually imperative that their experience of the therapist be explored. As with all therapeutic interventions, timing is vitally important. I thought L was ready, and I hoped such an exploration would open up the therapeutic space and make room for L to develop greater relatedness with me.

With an eating-disordered patient, the attempt is to tenaciously redirect the patient out of the world of food and into the arena of human interaction.

—Jean Petruccelli, *Treating Eating Disorders*

L was indeed ready, and she began to communicate this through the content of her derivatives even before I introduced the subject. She began to discuss makeup (L loved makeup). It was one of her favorite items for which to shop. She had just come from Sephora, a cosmetics store, and she showed me what she had purchased. I looked at the items with interest, but I was also busy thinking about what L was communicating by sharing them with me. I was curious, and after thanking her for showing me the items, inquired, "I am wondering if you are trying to tell me something?" L thought for a moment, and hesitantly stated, "Well, I noticed you don't wear makeup, and you should. You would look better." I opened up the therapeutic space for more exploration. "Have you had any other thoughts about my appearance?" I wondered. L replied, "Well, you always look nice, but you shop at Express, I can tell. I would never shop there. You should be wearing more expensive clothes." There was devaluation and criticism in her tone, but I did not feel angry or defensive.

I wondered with L whether she had thoughts about my body. Aside from being taller, L and I had similar body types I am thin and lean, but muscular, like L had been at her healthy weight. L remarked, "You are thin. Not as thin as I am now, but you are tall, so you don't have to diet." I began to feel her envy, and I also sensed some loathing from her body language and intonation. "Is it hard for you to see me as someone who doesn't have to diet?" I asked, recalling that L had been envious of the girls in her dorm who "could eat whatever they wanted." "No," L replied, but I sensed that this wasn't true. I believed that L devalued other aspects of my appearance to help her deal with the envy and rage she felt about confronting my body in the room. She was affectively restrictive, and was unable to experience her full range of emotions.

She then asked me if I was in a relationship. "I noticed you don't wear a wedding ring," she said. "You should be married by now." I did not feel that answering this question would be helpful to L, although I must admit that because of the hostility in her voice, I was very tempted to tell her that yes, indeed, I lived with my boyfriend, thank you very much. Instead, I inquired what it would mean to L if I were in a relationship. She remarked, "I would feel better. You should be."

L then displaced her rage toward me onto her roommate, who was also in a serious relationship. L felt rejected by this roommate, who spent most of her free time with her boyfriend, and, for the most part, only stopped at the dorm for changes of clothing. I imagined that L actually hoped I was also alone. From these exchanges, I learned the extent of L's envy and rage, which I believed grossly affected her ability to relate to her peers. I also recognized that her depreciation of me simultaneously deflected her envy and placed me in the role of the criticized child, which she usually occupied. In fact, as treatment progressed, L directed many devaluating remarks towards me. When I probed L for her thoughts about these comments, she denied any negative affect towards me.

L's emotional world was so impoverished that I believed her to be alexithymic—she had no words to describe her affect, especially when such an admission might threaten the integrity of an important relationship. She communicated what she felt through her actions, and I often felt as if I were the criticized and controlled child, who could not find any way out.

L continued to describe wanting a boyfriend. She shared endless stories of the attention she was finally receiving from men. She felt good, admired, and desirable, but despite positive feedback about her appearance, L's exchanges with men never led anywhere. "Why do my friends have boyfriends?" she would ask, envious and frustrated. We explored the possibility that the way she really felt about herself might be affecting her interactions with men. These feelings, we discussed, were deeply buried, but we needed to address them in our therapy.

We spent many sessions exploring L's feelings about herself, aside from her feelings about her physical appearance. This was quite difficult for her, as I knew it would be, but I pushed her, and encouraged her to explore her feelings about her inner being. I encouraged her to explore her needs (which was difficult, because she felt that she "shouldn't" have any), desires, and aspirations. Our path of inquiry was truly exhausting, because L was so fixated on her outward appearance. Her weight had risen slightly by this time, and had settled at about ninety pounds. Although she knew that she had had to increase her weight for health reasons, she was deeply distressed about her weight gain, and she still was not menstruating.

I again began to receive frantic messages from L's mother. Although I understood her anxieties, her intrusions angered me. I shared this with L, and inquired about her father's role. L had never talked about her father. She now described him as sympathetic toward her situation, but added, "My mother controls everything, even him." We worked together to help L set appropriate boundaries with her mother. They had been arguing more often, because of L's attempts to separate and establish some independence. I believed that Mrs. W's frenetic telephone messages had more to do with L's beginning to assert some independence than with her actual eating disorder again, food had become a symbol in this family's method of communication. L asserted herself, and with great effort was able to convince her mother to stop calling me. This was progress for L, and I was proud of her.

It was now L's senior year of college, and she felt the internal pressure of applying to graduate school. L wanted to apply for a master's degree program in journalism, but her mother discouraged her. "Stay home and find a job where you will make money. You can't handle the pressure of graduate school, especially with your condition," her mother would repeatedly remark. L, stronger now, confronted her mother about these critical statements, and insisted that she would attend graduate school with or without her mother's support.

One afternoon, L came into session glowing and happy, which was highly unusual (though she had been looking better, having reached a weight of ninety-five pounds). She had met a "boy" at school, and he had asked her out on a date. They would be going out on Friday night. L was overjoyed, and she told me about the boy, E. They shared a class, and had been flirting a bit over the last few months. He was a pre-med major, and "very hot." I encouraged her to explore her feelings about the upcoming date. I inquired, "Are you anxious at all?" More in touch with her feelings now, L replied, "Yes, I am." She explored the various possibilities that might arise during the course of the date. He wanted to go for a drink and then to dinner, both of which were activities that L forbade herself from enjoying. I tilted my head and looked at her curiously. More engaged in therapy now, L knew what I was thinking. "I know," she responded. "I never drink, and going to dinner is frightening for me, but I am going to do it. I like him." She practically waltzed out of session that day. I thought about L all weekend, and couldn't wait until our next session to find out how the date had gone. I was so excited for her that I felt like a gossiping schoolgirl.

The following week, L strolled into session so radiantly that I imagined hearts floating above her head. I anxiously waited for her to start. "The date was amazing!" she exclaimed. She went on to describe the fun she and E had together; they had so much in common, and they spent the whole night talking and laughing. I inquired about the cocktails and the food. L described feeling more free with herself; she had drunk one cosmopolitan, and even had eaten a hamburger. They had scheduled another date for the following week, and E had already called L to say he had had a great time. L went on to discuss her mother's intrusions. L had told her mother about the date, and Mrs. W had immediately found fault with E. Having made great therapeutic strides by this time, L was furious, and spoke about how she had begun to feel that her mother didn't want her to be happy.

As our sessions continued, L and E's relationship began to get relatively serious. To her mother's dismay, L was planning to travel to Vermont for the weekend to meet E's family. We spent many sessions exploring the restrictions L had placed on her own sexuality. She and E had kissed, but E wanted more, and L was anxious and ambivalent about her willingness to be more open sexually. Interestingly, L dressed quite sexily, and I remarked one day on the incongruence between her physical presentation and her inner resistance to experiencing herself as a person who had sexual desires.

It became clear that L dressed provocatively to draw attention and admiration from men. She wanted to be sexually desired. However, she still saw herself as a twelve-year-old girl, and therefore as someone too young to be sexual. We worked hard to help L become more connected to her natural adult sexual desire. L never masturbated, had no sexual fantasies, and had difficulty imagining herself as an adult with sexual needs. I opened up the therapeutic space by encouraging L to be curious about her pronounced detachment from her sexual being. "It's like being hungry," she stated. "I don't even know when I'm hungry anymore. I don't know what my basic needs are." Such disconnectedness is common among eating disordered patients: as they alienate themselves more and more from the natural physiological state of hunger, they eventually lose the ability to recognize hunger.

L was accepted into graduate school, though I was dismayed to learn that she planned to live at home while completing her master's degree. We discussed the possibility of her living on campus, but L felt that she couldn't afford it. This may have been true, but I also felt that she needed to remain physically close to her mother as she was separating from her emotionally. Meanwhile, L and E's relationship continued to progress, and L was able to engage in some intimate touching. We explored her simultaneous enjoyment of and discomfort with this experience. L was trying very hard to connect emotionally with her physical and sexual desires, but it was a terrifying process. Developing her adulthood was the most frighteningly difficult experience for her.

L's weight had now increased to one hundred pounds; she looked great, and she finally began menstruating again. She shared her fears of becoming fat. L accepted her body at the one-hundred-pound mark, but continued dieting with the hope that her weight would not increase. I felt less worried about L's physical well-being, but her continued ruminations involving food persisted. She remained attached to her dysfunctional way of relating to food, despite her tremendous progress.

During her first year of graduate school, L's weight fluctuated between ninety-eight and one hundred and five pounds. We continued to process her fixation on food and dieting. L, who was now relating more with me, maintaining a serious relationship with a young man, and pursuing the graduate training she desired, still held steadfast to her relationship with food.

L decided to terminate treatment because she intended to transfer into another graduate school to be closer to E, who was attending medical school. She was a relatively healthy weight, and was now able to enjoy physical intimacy with E, although they had not engaged in intercourse because L planned on waiting until she was married. L had made tremendous progress in her ability to relate with others, and had even established some independence from her mother. However, her inner world remained very focused on her body and overall appearance. Despite being in a fulfilling relationship, she still desired additional affirmation of her attractiveness from other men. During our termination process, we discussed what she still needed to work on, and I was able to refer her to an eating disorder specialist near her new university.

Our last session together was very telling. L thanked me for all the help I had given her, and discussed the progress she had made. However, in contrast to my other termination experiences, I noticed an emotional vacancy in the room. I would miss seeing L, but the exchange between us lacked the intensity I was accustomed to feeling during a final session. It has been two years since our termination, and I wonder about L. I hope she continued with treatment, and has been able to deepen her relationship with her inner emotional world.

Chapter 6

"I Am Hungry. Will You Feed Me?"

The nothing which is the object of dread becomes, as it were, more and more a something.

—Søren Kierkegaard

On the morning of my first session with K, I woke up feeling anxious. From our brief initial phone call, I had learned that K sought therapy for help dealing with a number of recent losses, including the death of his mother. The short conversation affected me powerfully. I heard the sadness and grief in his voice, and experienced a real sense of lethargy and dysphoria immediately after hanging up the telephone.

I had worked with patients who had endured losses before, but something in K's tone really tugged at the core of my being. I had begun studying existentialism as an undergraduate, and had received a master's degree in existential and phenomenological psychology before earning my doctorate in clinical psychology. I was acutely aware of my own tremendous struggles with death anxiety. As I prepared for my first session with K, I wondered what our initial encounter would be like.

Wisdom does not lead to madness, nor denial to sanity: the confrontation with the givens of existence is painful but ultimately healing.

—Irvin Yalom, *Existential Psychotherapy*

K arrived, and I immediately sensed his anguish and heartache. After our initial introductions, he began to speak about the loss of his mother. She had died three months earlier, only one month after her diagnosis with pancreatic cancer. K felt grief stricken, lost, and alone. He described being unable to perform even the most routine activities. He was anhedonic, lethargic, and felt like dying himself, though he assured me he wasn't suicidal. When I inquired about his support system, he described conflict with his father, which obviously made things more difficult. It wasn't until a few months later that I would learn the extent of the conflict within their relationship. He did have some support from his older brother and his younger sister, with whom he was very close, but he stated, while trying to hold back tears, that "there is nothing like the love of a mother." I could feel myself choking up, but I was able to maintain my composure.

There was something so vulnerable and sensitive about K that I instantly felt like comforting and consoling him. I even felt myself wanting to reach out and touch him, in order to soothe his palpable pain. I realized that this likely was something that K wanted and perhaps even needed, but I also knew that a physical gesture would be inappropriate, particularly during a first session. Instead, I attempted to comfort him with soothing, empathic statements. He described the rapid progression of his mother's illness in vivid detail. "The last few days with her lying in bed, swollen, were horrible, and I can't get these thoughts out of my head," K tearfully explained. "I don't know how to go on from here." K's pain filled the room, and I uncharacteristically exceeded our scheduled session time by a number of minutes. I responded with empathy, and assured K that we would work together to help him get through this very difficult time. He seemed a bit better as we scheduled our next appointment. Upon his departure, I felt like crying. The next six years would be filled with some of the most heartbreaking and inspiring moments I have ever personally or professionally experienced.

The thing that gives our every move its meaning is always totally unknown to us.

—Milan Kundera, *The Unbearable Lightness of Being*

That which is ontologically closest and well known, is ontologically the farthest and not known at all.

—Martin Heidegger, *Being and Time*

K cancelled our second session. When he called me to reschedule for the following week, he provided an excuse for having been unable to meet. I sensed that K felt overwhelmed and frightened by having opened up during our first session, and that he needed some space before he could come back in. Such fears are common in patients who have difficulty trusting others and openly disclosing personal information, as well as in patients who have endured traumatic losses. I didn't explore the underlying reasons why K may have missed the session, but I did make a mental note of it.

K came in the following week, and directly disclosed how difficult it was for him to open up to people; as I had imagined, our first session had been very difficult for him. We discussed slowing down the process of his sharing intimate details and feelings, which is a technique I have often used with traumatized patients. As traumatized patients begin to disclose the details of their suffering, they become terrified, and the clinician must modulate the quantity and quality of their disclosures in order for them not to become re-traumatized. I would slowly learn that K had been through more trauma than I could have imagined.

To establish rapport with K and slow down the process, I began by asking him to tell me more about himself. He revealed that he was thirty-six, had grown up in Brooklyn with his parents, one elder brother, one younger sister, and one younger brother. He was of Irish Catholic lineage, but no longer identified with any religion. He had earned a bachelor's degree in social work, and had been working towards his master's degree when his mother fell ill.

K seemed to feel a bit more at ease in the session, and he began to disclose that he had a relatively extensive history of drug use, which had begun when he was twelve years old, and had used alcohol recreationally with some other boys in the neighborhood. Eventually, he began using pills and cocaine at approximately the age of eighteen. "Soon after high school," he explained. At around twenty years of age, K had begun to use crack, which, in time, led to three months in a rehabilitation and detoxification facility. K, averting his eyes in shame, admitted that he still drank recreationally and used crack occasionally, though he tried really hard not to.

I had many questions, but I knew I needed to move slowly, because K was very fragile. I did ask if he had any sense of what had caused him to begin using drugs. K paused for a few moments, and we sat in silence as I curiously observed him in quandary. After about four minutes, he looked me straight in the eyes and disclosed that an adult neighbor had sexually abused him from the time he was eight years old. His mother had finally ended the abuse by rescuing K from this man's garage when he was ten years old. K looked down, and we sat in silence again for a few moments. I validated how difficult it must have been for him to share this painful experience with me. I then wondered with K, "What was it like to share this with me?" He stated that he felt anxious and uncomfortable, but that he knew he had to talk about it in order to get better. "I have all these thoughts in my head about everything that has happened to me, and I know I have to talk about it. I have been holding things in my whole life," he said. The session ended, and K, seemingly relieved, thanked me and quickly departed.

For the first four months of treatment, K's attendance was sporadic. We explored his difficulties. With bittersweet authenticity, he shared that it was extraordinarily difficult for him to talk he genuinely wanted to, but it was terribly painful for him. We explored collaboratively what he imagined made talking so difficult. K was finally able to identify and articulate an immense shame and self-hatred, which was exacerbated by speaking about certain things aloud. On countless occasions, K's pain was so potent that I felt an urge to hug him and tell him everything was going to be all right. I knew that my desire to hug K communicated something important about what K needed, but it was too soon to share my experience, so I held it in abeyance until the timing was right. I also sensed (correctly, as I would soon find out), that there was much more to K's shame than his sexual abuse.

As treatment unfolded and K's attendance became more regular, I began to learn exactly how many agonizing experiences he had suffered, some of which primarily organized and defined K's core sense of self, and threatened his fundamental way of being.

The fact that millions of people share the same vices does not make these vices virtues, the fact that they share so many errors does not make the errors truths. And the fact that millions of people share the same form of mental pathology does not make these people sane.

—Erich Fromm, *The Sane Society*

In addition to the loss of his mother, K had endured two other major losses within the last three years. He began to share painful details about the loss of his significant other three years earlier. K's partner had passed away after a six-year battle with AIDS and secondary opportunistic diseases, during which K had been his primary caregiver. K described the horrible deterioration of his partner's health, to which he had to borne witness. Attempting to hold back tears, he shared that he was still not over it. "I can't get the images of his being sick out of my head," he stated. I sensed resignation and helplessness in his tone. K's was homosexual and HIV-positive; I would soon learn that these were the primary sources of his shame.

As treatment continued, K began to disclose ways that his father had rejected and devaluated him because of his sexual orientation. Upon first learning of his son's homosexuality, K's father had dismissed him, and refused to acknowledge this fundamental part of his son's identity. Over time, and with the prodding of K's mother, K's father seemed to accept his son's sexual identity. However, he would intermittently make diminishing and shaming remarks, which left K unable fully to accept his own sexuality without experiencing excessive shame. Because of his father's insults, K now related to others and within his world from a centralized, fundamental, and primarily oriented sense of shame.

Shame is an emotional response to an attack on the global sense of self. When we are shamed, our very sense of who we are is threatened.

—Donald Dutton, *The Batterer*

K outwardly struggled with his sexual orientation and his HIV status. We spent many sessions focusing on K's anger surrounding being HIV-positive. Partially because of his father's attacks, he blamed himself for having lived his life in a way that left him vulnerable to contracting this disease. There were times that K would stop taking his medication, in self-retaliatory anger for having contracted HIV. We worked hard to reorganize K's way of thinking about his status and to create a less toxic self-image, and we explored the possibility that his self-hatred had resulted from the internalization of his father's imposed ideals, rather than from K's own values. K was a kind, gentle, but troubled soul, and my heart really went out to him.

In our second year of treatment, we continued to work on K's difficulty and discomfort discussing clinically relevant material. He was relatively well related, and when discussing less intense material, he was very comfortable and alive. However, when more significant, painful material would come up during our sessions, I noticed that he would become anxious and want to leave early. We were both acutely aware that it was extraordinarily difficult for K to sit with his feelings. We explored this many times, but I never pushed him; his sensitivity, gentleness, and vulnerability permeated the room.

K eventually disclosed that he had also lost his younger brother to a "hit and run" car accident approximately one year before his mother had died. K had witnessed the accident, and blamed himself for not being able to save his brother. Again, the potency of his pain filled the room; I wanted to cry, and a tear slowly ran down my face. I don't think K noticed, and if he did, he did not mention it. Had he commented, I might have started bawling. I wondered, many times, what it was about K that touched me so deeply. It was obvious to me that something co-created within our dyad connected us in a profound way, but at this time, it remained obscure. I did recognize this as important information, and often contemplated it during and after our sessions. During one session, it finally struck me: K had been so fundamentally deprived of unconditional love and nurturing that his need to feel loved, mirrored, and cared for was palpable. I could feel it without his communicating it directly. My own responses towards K provided this significant clinical information. My feelings wanting to take care of K, to "mother" him had developed because of his needs, and reflected the extent of his deprivation.

Approximately six months later, something horrible and unthinkable would happen that would intensify the unspoken connection between us. By this time, K's attendance had become consistent, and at his suggestion, we began to explore increasing our sessions to twice a week. Usually, I do prefer to work with patients twice or even three times a week, but I had been hesitant about pursuing such a schedule with K. I was uncertain about his ability to tolerate more frequent sessions, because he found it so difficult to sit with his feelings. After a month of processing, during which I shared my hesitancy, we decided collaboratively to try holding sessions twice a week.

About two weeks into this new therapeutic frame, K began cancelling both sessions each week. "I knew he wasn't ready," I thought, as K communicated his fears through action. I knew K genuinely wanted to intensify our alliance and work together, but it was too soon; he was still too uncomfortable. I had hoped to process K's fears and discomfort during our session, but he simply would not come in. I was left with only the much less desirable option of discussing his ambivalence by telephone. Aware of his anxieties, K acquiesced, and we decided to move temporarily back to weekly sessions, with the intention of attempting to increase to twice-weekly sessions again after K became more comfortable. K resumed attending sessions regularly following our talk (and this is a valuable example of how sensitively clinicians must evaluate each patient's unique ability to intensify the therapeutic process).

About two months later, and after processing K's discomfort and self-hatred more intensely, we were able to resume twice-weekly sessions; by this time, K had become more able to tolerate discomfort and sit with difficult feelings, and he attended sessions regularly. This was major progress for K.

A denial of death at any level is a denial of one's basic nature and begets an increasingly pervasive restriction of awareness and experience. The integration of the idea of death saves us; rather than sentence us to existences of terror or bleak pessimism, it acts as a catalyst to plunge us into more authentic life modes, and it enhances our pleasure in the living of life.

—Irvin Yalom, *Existential Psychotherapy*

We had been seeing each other twice a week for about three months, and working hard to diminish K's self-hatred and his internalizations of his father's shaming insults. Then, it happened.

My mother hadn't been feeling well for a few months, and her doctors were having difficulty figuring out what was wrong. She had excessive stomach pains, loss of appetite, reflux, back pain, and fatigue. It was terrifying, and I sensed that that this unnamed assailant of my mother's well being was serious. We finally learned how serious. As my cherished mother's health began quickly and frighteningly to deteriorate, she received a diagnosis: pancreatic cancer. Though I knew the prognosis wasn't good, I grasped for some hope. But as Mom's health rapidly declined, and the doctors informed us that the cancer was at such a late stage that there was nothing they could do but make her more comfortable, my hope transformed into devastation. As I watched Mom weaken and become swollen, I thought of K's comment during our initial session: "There is nothing like the love of a mother."

Mom, vibrant, loving, and just shy of her sixty-fourth birthday, died only one month following her diagnosis, just as K's mother had. Now, I too suffer vivid and intrusive memories of my mother lying motionless, bloated, and unable to eat or even sit up on her own. I remember feeling depersonalized (a common psychological defense against trauma) during her funeral. I saw Mom's name in front of the ceremony room, and yet was unable to process that "Rochelle Simon" was really my mother, and that this funeral was Mom's funeral. This experience has forever changed me.

Psychology is one of the most fascinating and exhilarating professions one can choose. However, clinicians often face complex and intricate dilemmas, and must make decisions quickly in uncertain circumstances, remaining ever mindful of the possible consequences to and effects on our patients. I found myself in one of these predicaments while dealing with the profound hardship of losing my mother. I had to call my patients and inform them that I would be cancelling sessions for two weeks, without revealing my bereavement or my immense grief. I called all my patients with the same flat explanation: "I am fine, but I have a family emergency and will be out of the office for two weeks." I provided each patient with a covering clinician's contact information, and, thankfully, none asked directly what happened. Many of my patients wanted reassurance that I was fine, to which I responded that I was, but that was all.

Two weeks later, still in a pronounced stupor of sadness and grief, I returned to work. Patients usually react intensely to such breaks in the frame, and I was anxious about the reactions and questions I might have to negotiate. Remarkably, my patients did not ask where I had been or what happened. They did not act out, nor did they seem to question our sudden break in the derivatives of their content. Most patients were simply relieved to see that I was "fine." I certainly wasn't "fine" I felt as though I would never be "fine" again but I was able to hold myself together. I imagined that my patients might have sensed intuitively that they should not question or retaliate against whatever had taken me away for two weeks. Perhaps they recognized that I was suffering. I was extremely relieved by their cooperation, but it remains a mystery to me even now.

As I continued working with K, I felt myself wanting to share with him that I also had just lost my mother. However, I needed to understand what this desire meant. Did I want K to comfort me? This would clearly contraindicate a disclosure, as it would seriously violate a boundary. For nearly two months, I pondered my quandary, and I felt my desire to share my experience during every session with K.

Eventually, I concluded that sharing my story of loss with K might help him to feel more comfortable and understood, and would make him feel safer discussing painful topics with me. We had developed an excellent rapport, but K was still uncomfortable speaking about painful issues. I hoped, by disclosing that we in fact shared a strikingly similar heartbreak, to open the therapeutic space for K to articulate his own feelings surrounding the losses he had suffered.

Understanding my reasoning, and feeling that my disclosure was in K's best interest, I waited patiently for an appropriate opening. A few sessions later, K began to speak about his mother. When he finished, and after a pause, I gently stated, "There is something I would like to share with you. How do you feel about that?" K responded with concern, "What is it? Are you okay?" I reassured him that I was OK, and then began to share my mother's recent diagnosis and death with him. K listened attentively, with what appeared to be almost disbelief. When I finished, he looked down and stated, "I am sorry.

Thank you for telling me." We sat in a comfortable silence for a few moments. I sensed an intimacy between us, a shared understanding, as we each sat with our own feelings of loss. K then began to share his feelings surrounding the loss of his mother in more elaborate detail than he had used thus far in our treatment. He appeared more free, more related, and more comfortable. I knew then that disclosing my own experience had been the right thing to do.

Following my disclosure, sessions with K intensified; I sensed that he had become more connected to his affect and had, for the first time, experienced truly empathic sharing. It wasn't simply the content of my disclosure, but the fact that I trusted him and our relationship enough to be so open with him, that provided him with a "corrective emotional experience" (*i.e.*, he experienced something he hadn't experienced before—authentic relating and this was curative). He began discussing his self-hatred more frequently and openly, and through his cadence and overall appearance, he seemed more comfortable with his fundamental identity.

Incidentally, K was quite attractive. He had a tall, strong stature, dark brown hair, and soft brown eyes. As his self-hatred became less intense, his skin had grown more vibrant, and he was almost glowing. I noticed this with him, and he clearly was moved by my noticing him and by the experience of being seen not as a gay, HIV-positive man, but as a whole and worthy person who deserved honest, reciprocal interactions.

We were now close to the beginning of our fourth year of treatment, and K was doing quite well. His self-hatred had diminished dramatically, and he was even contemplating returning to school. Unfortunately, K's father now began to verbally degrade K's lifestyle more excessively than usual. K even described subtle rejections from his siblings. His feelings of self-worth still new and untested, K began to isolate himself, and described a rebound of dysphoric mood, which sounded more serious than his previous episodes of depression. He even cancelled a few sessions. I became concerned and began to wonder if I was going to have to hospitalize K.

After four successive cancellations, K finally came to session. I was relieved to see him, but I had an ominous feeling once he sat down, and I thought, sadly, that I would have to hospitalize him. I had just completed this thought when K blurted out, "Jacquie, I feel suicidal. I want to go to the hospital." I was disconcerted, but I also felt proud of K; he knew he needed help, and he had clearly articulated this need. I called K's psychiatrist, who was affiliated with a nearby hospital, and K was immediately admitted. K remained in the hospital for three weeks until he stabilized, his mood improved, and he no longer manifested suicidal ideation.

During the first week of his hospitalization, K called me frequently, and after some deliberation, I decided to visit him. Aside from showing genuine concern, such visits can often help patients to reorganize and stabilize, though clinicians must assess each patient individually. I decided that visiting K was the right thing to do.

K was a cigarette smoker. He had quit, on and off, throughout our treatment together, but at the time of his hospitalization, he was smoking, and of course smoking is prohibited in the hospital. During one of our telephone conversations prior to my visit, K talked about his nicotine patch and complained, "I can't smoke. The least they could do is have good coffee. The coffee here is nasty." I knew K loved coffee; he often talked about his espresso machine, and he usually arrived at our sessions with a Starbucks coffee in his hand. After some thought, I decided that I would bring him some coffee when I visited. Though we often hear that it is "the thought that counts," this sentiment does not adequately address the action of a clinician giving something material to a patient. Every act of giving is a unique communication within the co-created therapeutic dyad. By bringing K a simple cup of coffee, I would be communicating that I, unlike his father and other relatives, had heard and acknowledged his need, that I wanted to ease it, and that this was a reasonable expectation for him to have of the people around him. I wanted K to realize that he was a worthy individual, important enough to deserve concrete validation of his needs.

When I arrived at the hospital and gave K his coffee, he was surprised and delighted. "No one has ever done anything like this for me before. Thank you," he said graciously. This reaction moved me, I could feel tears welling up in my eyes. A few days later, I returned with another cup of coffee. Once K was discharged from the hospital, and after he had become more emotionally stable, we processed his experience of receiving the coffee. As I had hoped, K reported that it was the first time anyone had really met his needs without his having to ask for something. In that moment, I again wanted to hug him he was so gentle and sweet, and yet so deprived and wounded.

A few months following K's hospitalization, I bought a coffee pot for my office. I was so busy with patients and supervisees that I often did not have enough time to go to the kitchen and make coffee. I began to notice that I would make coffee for K before our sessions. If there was no coffee already in the pot as K's appointment time approached, I would make some specifically for him. I also noticed that I had begun to offer him some of the cashews that I regularly snacked on throughout the day. Uncharacteristically, I hadn't engaged in any forethought before these actions I simply realized

I was performing them, and then began to wonder why. At first, I thought that perhaps I was simply trying to make our sessions more comfortable. This was partially true, but did not feel entirely right. As I continued to process my actions, I finally realized that I was *feeding* K. I was attempting to feed him as a mother does her child. Becoming the mother that K had lost, and simultaneously identifying with my own lost mother, I was providing love, and nurturing K, by giving him coffee and snacks. I thought it was important to articulate and process these actions with K, but I felt that the time was not right. I wasn't sure K was quite ready to explore the amount of emotional deprivation he had experienced. I continued to feed him.

I was surprised when K began to disclose that his mother also had difficultly accepting his homosexuality. It is often difficult for a patient to experience normal ambivalence toward a deceased parent, particularly if the lost parent was thought of as kinder or more sympathetic than the other. K's revelation of this trait of his mother's showed tremendous progress and courage. As he began to further explore some of the rejections he had felt from his mother, he began to eat the cashews very quickly, feeding himself, as an antidote to the painful material he found himself revealing. Together, we explored his feelings. He was on the verge of tears, but continued to work hard to contain himself. "It is okay to cry in here. What stops you?" I asked. K responded, "I know. It is very hard for me. I have always held everything in." At this point, I began to explore the "feeding" with K, and what it might mean about what I sensed he needed. K was able to hear and accept this, and he began to discuss the extent of his deprivation in more detail. I did continue to provide him with coffee. Though complex dynamics had created my desire to feed K, and we were now exploring his lifetime of emotional deprivation for the first time in our therapy, the feeding had become a part of our human connection I felt that it would be a mistake to take it away.

K and I are still working together in twice-weekly sessions. He has made immense strides in his treatment. We have a strong working alliance, and K is more comfortable speaking openly in sessions. He has developed an observing ego, and his self-hatred has diminished significantly. He continues to work on establishing a firm sense of self that is not defined by his internalization of painful insults and shame, and that integrates his lifestyle, life experiences, and unique and special qualities. I continue to feed him coffee and cashews.

Chapter 7

"The Naughty Little Boy"

Eros moves in many different directions, so that the worlds of fantasy generated each has its own erotic delights. The Eros of one may seem perverted and perverting to the other.

—Thomas Moore, *Dark Eros*

Immediately upon his arrival to our first session, M emphatically stated, "I cannot achieve sexual satisfaction through mutual involvement." M's complete lack of emotion while making this declaration was remarkable, and later became an essential theme throughout our therapy. Usually, patients present with varying levels of distress surrounding the issues that have brought them into therapy. M showed no distress at all. In fact, as our twice-weekly therapy unfolded over six years, M introduced me to his abundant erotic fantasies, his childhood traumas, and his unconventional lifestyle, all with this same incredible disconnectedness.

M was thirty-nine years old, and had been raised by his single mother. His father had left his mother for another woman when M was two years old, and M reported no memory of him. His mother, now in her eighties, had moved to Florida when M was thirty-five. M was completing his PhD in Social Psychology, and lived alone in Manhattan. "Alone" is a somewhat paradoxical description of M, because his internalization of his provocative and seductive mother was so pronounced that it seemed that he carried her with him always.

During the beginning stages of our treatment, M vividly recounted the many boundary betrayals he had experienced during childhood. He portrayed his mother, his primary and only caretaker, as controlling and overpowering. He described overwhelming instances where she would "play with him" in what he now believed were inappropriate ways. He stated that his mother had "controlled [his] body."

M's mother had bathed him until he was approximately fifteen years old. M described enjoying the baths in his earlier years, but as he began puberty, M had expressed confusion and discomfort with bath time. However, M explained that he had no choice in the matter, and that his mother did not respect his boundaries or his need for privacy, and continued to perform the baths as a perfunctory part of each day. As therapy progressed, M began to reveal that he felt erotically stimulated by the baths, yet simultaneously disgusted by his own arousal.

In addition, M had "played" with his mother by exposing his genitals to her well into his early twenties. She would usually respond by swatting his derriere, and she never once insisted that he cover himself, or suggested that his behavior was inappropriate. She "played back," M explained, by walking around the house naked at her leisure. Such boundary violations as these can be equally or more damaging than overt incest, because they are insidious and confusing. For example, M remained unclear about how much of their "play" had been inappropriate until he had moved out of his mother's house at the age of twenty-six and had begun researching sexual abuse. Until this time, he had merely questioned whether this was the way all boys related to their mothers.

Consistent with M's overall way of being-in-the-world and of relating to others, M described feeling angry with his mother for her betrayals, but exhibited no affect connected to the emotions that he articulated. M was intellectually brilliant, and during this early stage of treatment, I hypothesized that he was using his intellect to defend himself against feeling intense rage toward his mother. Such rage would mean a separation from her, and theirs was clearly a deeply enmeshed relationship from which disengagement would prove an extreme challenge.

Betrayal is a violation not only of trust and of the other, but the sanctity of intimate relationships An implicit covenant has been broken or denied It changes something fundamental; a belief or a frame of reference from which to view the world of interpersonal relationships.

—Olga Cheselka, *Betrayal: Common and Extraordinary*

Throughout our treatment together, M continually returned to thoughts, images, and fantasies about his complex relationship with his mother. As our relationship progressed, he began to disclose an inner world filled with erotic fantasies involving sadomasochism, exhibitionism, and pedophilia. I would later learn that he often acted on his sadomasochistic and exhibitionist fantasies, and usually achieved orgasm through these actions. However, his pedophiliac fantasies were ego-dystonic and distressing to M, and he kept them strictly under control.

It was clear to me that M's fantasies and his propensity to act on them, as well as his inability to experience an orgasm through mutual sexual relations, were related to his early betrayals. M was able to make these connections intellectually, and, in fact, spoke incessantly about the association. However, despite this insight, he showed little distress about his fantasies and behaviors. In fact, as treatment progressed, I began to experience M's sharing of his lifestyle with me as a sort of exhibitionism, and I wondered if he was aroused by our therapy. It was too early in our treatment to address this relational component, though I believed that the therapy needed to move in this direction. Temporarily, I kept my experience of him to myself.

M slowly began vividly to describe his experiences in the sadomasochistic community. He was very involved in wax burning, and shared stories about his engagement in these rituals. M went to clubs where he would either witness others drip hot wax onto a woman or drip the wax onto her himself. At times, he would volunteer to have wax dripped onto him. Following this ritual, he would either masturbate in the club, or rush home to masturbate in his apartment.

M described having no preference for participating as the sadist or as the masochist, and described both roles as equally arousing. I believed that this reflected his sense of alienation and his detachment from his conflicts surrounding the power dynamics with his mother, which were the origin of his propensity to engage in and become aroused by these encounters.

I was unsure about how best to process M's inner world to establish uniqueness in our therapeutic relationship. I needed to discern what therapeutic position would provide the best technique to help M. Should I understand M's fantasy world and lifestyle as a symptom? Or should I recognize that this was not aberrant behavior for M, but rather a unique mode of expression for his sexuality? Since his fantasies and lifestyle seemed syntonic (without distress), I decided to proceed from the latter position.

From a phenomenological perspective, the notion of *eros*, the root of *erotic*, does not define correct or incorrect erotic impulses in response to certain objects. From this perspective, sadomasochism is understood as an *a priori* human possibility, and only requires analysis if it causes psychic distress. Since M did not experience any distress surrounding this channel for his erotic impulses, I chose to validate M's sadomasochistic fantasies. However, he did express distress, if only intellectually, surrounding his inability to perform in a conventional and mutual relationship. I did encourage M to be curious about the possible connections between the two. I felt if he were to become able to integrate his sadomasochism with his conventional sexual ideals, he might become more able to perform in a mutual relationship.

Having resolved my own internal quandary, our treatment continued, and slowly unfolded into a very complex, and, at times, quite difficult therapy. M gradually continued to reveal more and more about his participation in the sadomasochistic community, such as his experiences with aggressive tickling. During one of our sessions, M revealed that he was on his way to a tickling convention for the weekend. Prior to this session, he had not discussed his affinity for aggressive tickling. He described his involvement with a community of people who participated in tickling each other to the point of painful breathlessness. As with his passion for wax burning, M enjoyed the roles of both tickler and ticklee. He glowed with excitement about the upcoming weekend. Once again, I wondered whether part of his exhilaration came from his experience of disclosing such things to me.

At around the same time, M began to discuss his foot fetish. I looked down at my open-toed shoes as he began to describe the delight and arousal he found in fondling a woman's feet. Upon further exploration, he described being primarily aroused by the odor of a woman's foot. He particularly enjoyed the stench of a sweaty foot; M was more stimulated by a woman's foot after she had been wearing boots all day, for example. He indulged me with stories about the "foot play" in which he frequently engaged with a female friend, who would remove her boots, and give him her feet to play with as the sweaty odor filled the room.

We explored collaboratively, with M's lead, what the foot might have represented metaphorically. M was able to associate his childhood shame experiences with his erotic desire for the foot. M enjoyed his fetish, but he did begin to question ways that early experiences of shame, humiliation, and helplessness at the hands of his mother might have contributed to his erotic desire to be humiliated by smelling a malodorous foot.

As treatment progressed, M began to focus on trying to meet a woman with whom he could develop an intimate relationship. We spoke at length, again with M's lead, about how he might fit his lifestyle into a possible relationship. He also began to become more cognizant of his fear of women. M feared that he would experience the same sense of powerlessness with a romantic partner that he had experienced with his mother. This was a major step forward in M's treatment until now, he had been unaware of this conflict. He was, however, unable to attach any affective expression of anger or rage towards his mother to this realization.

At this point, I decided to process this resistance with M, and we explored what it might mean for him to experience anger towards his mother. Surprisingly, he was able to work with this supposition. He feared that his anger would devour and destroy her, and therefore, he felt that he had to shut himself off from his feelings. I also believed that he was afraid that his anger would precipitate a separation from her, which would leave him fragmented and disorganized, because so much of his identity rested on his internalizations of his mother.

M's early and brutal betrayals by his mother had created the foundation for his current experience of intimate relationships. His fears of powerlessness and helplessness reflected his internalization of his toxic relationship with his mother, which was the origin of his early identity formation. I began to speculate about how this internalization might be manifesting in our therapeutic relationship. Importantly, I felt no power struggle or eroticism unfolding between us. As clinicians, we use our own emotional experiences within the therapeutic dyad as vital clinical material; our reactions intuitively inform us of our patients' inner experiences and reveal emotional material that patients cannot articulate. I began to look for openings to process the relational component of our shared experience in the therapy room with M.

The opening I had been waiting for came up a few sessions later when M reported the following dream:

> I was in the library working on my dissertation research. I had to make copies. While I was waiting for the copy machine, you walked in. I was glad to see you and walked over to say hello. I imagined you would be pleased to see me there, and I was excited to have a conversation with you, but you brushed past me, barely noticing my presence.

Holding my own thoughts about his dream in abeyance, I asked M for his associations. He began to discuss having had experiences with women in the library akin to my interaction with him in the dream. He described feeling humiliated on a number of occasions when he had innocuously approached women at school to initiate conversations, and had been met by indifference and discomfort, which had been communicated through these women's body language.

Using these derivatives as an opening to discuss our relationship, I began to probe M about his experience of me. In response to my inquiry, M began a long discourse about his images of two different types of women. He depicted one group as the awkward type, whom he experienced as similar to himself and thus less threatening. He described the second group as popular and unattainable women, about whom he fantasized from afar and would occasionally approach, only to be rejected. This was the first time that I had sensed some emotion from M; his intonation and facial expression reflected shame and rage. He quickly regained his composure, and returned to his distancing intellectual defenses.

M continued associating his experiences with these two groups of women with similar experiences he had had with women in high school and college. He discussed his proclivity to spend a great deal of time, sometimes hours, watching these elusive, and, he admitted, ultimately threatening women, from a safe distance. He eventually was able to process his rage towards them as representatives of a generalized woman who had rejected him and left him feeling humiliated. Although this diatribe expressed important clinically relevant material, it enabled M to avoid having to deal with his complex feelings towards me or towards his mother.

I decided to give M a slight clinical push by connecting his dream about me with his overall images of women. This time, I directly questioned my place within these symbols, and M was receptive. He described imagining our relationship, under different circumstances, as that of cohorts; he fantasized that we were graduate students together, studying and bouncing ideas off of each other. He further portrayed me as part of the "in crowd," but imagined that I would accept him, just as I did in our therapeutic interactions. Extrapolating from M's dream and the associations that followed, I believed that M's relational content exhibited his need to protect me from his rage. Though I did indeed embrace M's uniqueness in therapy, his elaborate inner world demonstrated that M was not able to experience rejection from me at this time. Any experience of me as a person who might humiliate or overpower him was far too threatening. Any sharing or interpretations of these contradictory images of me would be premature, so I again held back from further exploration at this time.

I began to notice that I drank more coffee than usual before and during our sessions. Although the content that M brought in was fascinating and provocative, I often found myself uncharacteristically sleepy during our sessions, because of his inclination to create distance between the conversation, its emotional content, and his split-off rage. I knew the next step forward with M was gently to start creating curiosity about his propensity to distance himself and isolate his cognitions from his affect states. Until M could integrate his images, fantasies, and intellectual ideas with their corresponding difficult emotional experiences, his identity formation (which rested largely on his internalization of his early relationship with his mother) would not change.

M came into our next session and announced that he would be missing our sessions the following week because he was going away to a nudist retreat. Prior to this revelation, I had not known that M was part of a nudist community. He excitedly described previous experiences at these retreats, and was quite animated during our discussion. I pointed out his enthusiasm and expressed curiosity. M explained that he felt comfortable among the people he met at these retreats. He described a lack of pretense in the community, and revealed that he felt less awkward approaching "in-crowd women" in the nudist environment.

M also claimed that he felt no erotic arousal associated with being a nudist. He did not feel aroused by exposing himself, nor did he experience any erotic feelings when he saw others exposed. However, he did divulge that publically exposing himself *as* a nudist aroused him; that is, M became erotically stimulated when he shared with others that he was a nudist. I wondered with M what it was like for him to tell me about this part of his life. He admitted that it was arousing. "What about it is arousing?" I asked. M described feeling like a "naughty little boy," which was akin to his simultaneous feelings of arousal and disgust that surrounded the "play" in which he had engaged with his mother.

As we were processing his experience of disclosing this intimate material to me, I began to experience M, for the first time, as a "naughty little boy." As he sat in his chair across from me, I intuitively and suddenly began to see him as the "naughty little boy" he had internalized from his childhood. This image of M disgusted me, which made me very uncomfortable, because I usually experience empathy towards my patients. To help M, I had to separate myself from this feeling of disgust, so that I might understand what it truly communicated. As I internally processed the session, it finally became clear to me that I had actually felt what M had felt during his childhood interactions with his provocative and seductive mother. I had felt M's concomitant arousal (even my heart rate had increased) and disgust.

Although projective identification is a disorienting, deeply disturbing experience for the clinician, it is also, like dissociation, an invaluable venue for communicating information about the self that is intolerable for the patient to consciously know about and express.

> —Jody Davies and Mary Frawley, *Treating the Adult Survivor of Childhood Sexual Abuse: A Psychoanalytic Perspective*

M returned from his retreat exhilarated and full of stories to share and process. He felt particularly that the interactions he had had with a certain woman would provide significant clinical material. He revealed that they had danced intimately (while naked, of course), and that he had become sexually aroused by the closeness. Though they had only danced, this was the first time that M had been able to become erect with a woman without sadomasochism or fetishism. He was also very excited that this woman had clearly felt his erectness and had not snubbed or rejected him, but also had seemingly been aroused by the shared intimacy. This was tremendous progress for M. He had, for the first time, felt safe enough to allow himself to feel vulnerable and close to a woman.

We explored what this experience meant to him. I also opened up the therapeutic space by probing M for his fantasies about what it might have been like if any further intimacies had occurred with this woman, S. M immediately responded by returning to defensive intellectualizations of his fantasies. He did describe imagining that he might be able to perform in consensual sex that would end in orgasm, but his narrative was vacant and emotionless. With some internal hesitation, I took this lead. I noted and was curious with M about his disconnection from what would otherwise seem to be emotionally charged clinical material, and I finally confronted him with his tendency to isolate his cognitions from complex, affectively charged material. The session ended with M's repeating, "Emotion, emotion. I will have to think about that."

"Emotion," M immediately stated at the beginning of our next session. M maintained excellent continuity between our sessions, which implied that he spent time thinking about our time together, and suggested that M was able to internalize the therapeutic relationship. This capacity is not only a strength, but is an essential part of successful therapy.

M was really struggling to understand why it was so difficult for him to experience emotion. I intuitively sensed that M was not being defensive or resistant, but that he truly was dissociated from his emotional experience. M's history of covert sexual abuse left him susceptible to dissociation, which had been M's only way of surviving the abuse. I shared my thoughts with

M. We explored the process of integrating dissociative material. It was very challenging to avoid joining M in his intellectualizations, because I also tend to intellectualize. We discussed that it was now necessary for M to deeply process his painful experiences, learn to articulate them, and, most importantly, integrate the experiences with his articulations, so that he might feel the pain that he had heretofore split off from his consciousness. I felt exhausted just thinking about helping M integrate his feelings. M had many strengths. I enjoyed working with him, I always looked forward to our sessions, but the extent to which he had cut himself off from his emotional world was challenging.

By this time, we were well into our fourth year of treatment together, and we spent many session hours discussing and exploring M's early experiences of his mother's betrayal. M worked hard to find words to describe his feelings. He gradually exhibited some integrated rage towards his mother because she had violated his boundaries and left him feeling powerless in their relationship. He also spoke at length about his fears of re-experiencing powerlessness and helplessness in an intimate relationship with a woman. M slowly and arduously began to understand his inability to perform as a somatic, and double-edged, communication. M felt emasculated, powerless, and immobilized by the prospect of performing sexually with a woman. Paradoxically, he was simultaneously afraid of his own masculinity and power, which, if expressed, would separate him from his mother. This fear further paralyzed his ability to perform.

M and I discussed this interesting, yet agonizing, contradiction, and its manifestation in his enjoyment of both sadistic and masochistic roles. During these difficult sessions, M often returned to his defensive intellectualizations. Now, however, I stopped him, confronted his defenses, and became curious with him about which feeling was coming up and impeding his progress. By this time, M had become able to access, or at least articulate, the affect state that had prefaced his inclination to intellectualize.

Treatment seemed to be progressing quite well when M came to session and shared some rather disturbing pedophiliac fantasies. He discussed spending hours on the Internet, indulging his curiosity about men having sex with young children. M found his fascination with such acts extremely disturbing, and definitively stated that he would never act on them. Yet, pedophiliac thoughts often intruded upon his studies, and his absorption in these thoughts hindered him from completing his academic work in a timely fashion.

I wondered, "Why now?" Why, after almost five years of twice-weekly sessions, had M brought this material into therapy *now*? Many hypotheses ran through my head, but I decided to ask M directly. M revealed feeling indignity and shame about his vivid fantasy world, and I was able to experience his shame as he disclosed this affect state. He explained that he had finally felt safe enough in our relationship to share this distressing material, because he now knew that I would not judge him. M was right. As an experienced clinician who has been privy to many private and painful fantasies, I indeed listened without judgment. Instead, I integrated this material, and worked to understand what it meant in terms of M's characterological development.

Because M expressed profound unrest about his fantasies, it was best for us to access what they communicated about his overall development through collaboration and curiosity. Together, we began to connect M's childhood vulnerability and powerlessness to his interest in the penchants of adults who violated the purity and innocence of children, the same violation he had endured. After quite a few arduous sessions, M began to articulate his identification with these children. He expressed rage that his innocence had been stripped from him, and that he continued to suffer the consequences as an adult. After some time and hard work with this topic, M's compulsive urges to read about other men's experiences of molesting children subsided. This was a major step forward. M expressed pronounced relief and a newfound sense of control.

A few weeks after this breakthrough, M came in and reported the following dream:

> I was handcuffed to a bathtub. The tub had dirt and soap scum all around the sides. Some man gave me a sponge and some cleaner. I was scrubbing and scrubbing, but I couldn't get it clean.
> I woke up and felt very uncomfortable and dirty.

I felt M's shame permeating the room as he described the dream. I wondered if he too felt the shame that his unconscious had so cleverly symbolized while he slept. I probed M for associations. M associated the bathtub with his childhood and adolescent "bath time." The handcuffs, M continued, represented the helplessness he had felt while being bathed, and the way his mother had maintained control over his body. He started to become confused while exploring the possible meanings of the dirt and soap scum. I aided M by instructing him to process the dirt as a metaphor for the way he had felt during bath time. Strikingly, M was able to make the connection. He understood the dirt to represent the shame and humiliation he had felt surrounding the baths.

I pointed out to M that the dream was constructive, because in it, he was attempting to rid himself of his shame by cleaning the tub. This paralleled where we were in therapy; we were now working collaboratively to process M's shame, integrate it, and ultimately free him from it. The dream, and the discussion that followed, also suggested that M was finally beginning to separate from his long-standing identity organization around this fundamental shame. This was a major achievement for M, and I wondered if this would eventually help M with his presenting problem. Would this render M more likely to maintain and perform in a mutual relationship?

M did begin to bring in clinical material about some dates he had had with women he'd met on the Internet. This was promising, because M was now risking placing himself in situations where he might meet an appropriate mate. At this time, he was also working hard to finish his dissertation. M processed his risk-taking in the dating arena as an expression of his ability see himself finally as scholar (a role that he felt carried a sense of autonomy and power), rather than as a student.

M's dating experiences opened up the therapy for discussions about earlier incidents with woman during which he had been unable to perform. M had alluded to these previous occurrences in earlier sessions, but now he elaborated with candor and emotion. One notable instance had occurred with a woman he had been dating for four months during his junior year of college. M explained that this young woman had wanted to have sex early in their relationship, but that he had put it off. M now retrospectively understood that his modesty had reflected his larger fear of allowing himself to be open and vulnerable to this woman. At the time, he had only thought he was anxious about his ability to perform. M further explained that he often became erect while kissing and fondling this woman, but would immediately lose his erection upon feeling any unbridled and mutual passion beginning to evolve. For M, becoming uninhibited left him feeling helpless and out of control. The relationship ended abruptly, after one unforgettable night when M lost his erection just as he was about to enter her. She left, livid, referring to M as a "freak." M recalled feeling relieved as she stormed out the door.

We spent scores of sessions exploring M's desire to overcome his inhibitions in intimate situations. However, it was clear to me that M was still conflicted, because his relationships with potential partners would not go beyond the second date. His customary explanation was that the woman in question had been "too conventional." "An 'in crowd' woman," I began to point out. "The 'type' of woman who could possibly hurt and reject you." M heard and recognized my confrontation, and yet he continued to have trouble sustaining relationships beyond the second date. He did continue to date, however, and we continued to process his experiences, and, finally, his emotions.

M had remained quite involved with the sadomasochistic community, and he expressed some hope that he might meet a woman at one of the many events he attended. He did disclose a few instances in which he had met women via this avenue and had maintained somewhat ongoing relationships. These relationships usually involved his inviting the women to his apartment for red wine and "sadomasochistic play," which would ultimately result in mutual masturbation and orgasm. These experiences were congruent with M's desires, and he did receive gratification from them. However, he still hoped to one day engage in intimate, mutually satisfying intercourse.

We were well into our sixth year of treatment, and M had finally defended and deposited his dissertation. He would soon receive his degree, and he began searching for faculty positions throughout the country. We discussed the possibility of our prematurely terminating therapy should he get a job far from New York City. After a few months of interviewing, M accepted a tenure-track position in Indiana. I was delighted for M, but also saddened that our years of hard work would end soon, and well before I thought M was ready to terminate treatment.

During our three-month termination process, M expressed gratitude for the unconditional support he had received, and for the progress he had made. Though M had not yet engaged in mutually satisfying sex, his emotional world was more integrated, his sense of self no longer rested on deep-seated shame, and he was more aware of his conflicts about women. He also had become able to maintain more appropriate boundaries with his mother, and no longer felt like the helpless child he once had been. I referred M to a psychologist near the university where he would be teaching, and I hoped that with continued therapy, M would attain his goals and become able to have the relationship he wanted.

Our last session was quite powerful. I believe the potency of our six years together had deeply affected both of us. I was reasonably emotional, and I also felt the strength of M's emotions as we processed our years of work together. We hugged as we said our good-byes. I was deeply moved by this hug, and I thought about it for quite some time. I came to understand it as a symbolic communication of the appropriate boundaries that had been set forth within the therapeutic frame, of M's finally feeling safe enough to feel close to me. This, I thought, was promising.

Chapter 8

Hugs and Other Forms of Physical Touch

"Yes, I enjoyed hugging her. I like this lady a lot. She wears this incredible perfume. If I didn't enjoy it I wouldn't do it!"
"Oh? That's an interesting comment. I thought this avuncular hug was for the patient."
"It is. But if I didn't enjoy it, she'd sense it and the gesture would lose all authenticity."
"Talk about mumbo-jumbo!"

—Irvin Yalom, *Lying on the Couch*

One of my supervisees arrived for our weekly supervision meeting, and I immediately sensed some uncharacteristic uneasiness. "What happened?" I asked. He responded by sharing with me that he had just concluded his first session with a new patient, and that at the end of the session, the patient had hugged him. "There was no time to process the hug. It happened just as he was walking out the door. It made me really uncomfortable," he nervously recounted. Because this had been their first session, and we had no real sense or formulation of the patient, it was very difficult to gauge what the hug might have communicated. We did believe that the gesture was significant, because it is uncommon for a patient to hug his or her new therapist after a first session.

We explored the possible meanings of the hug by focusing on my supervisee's intuitive sense of the patient. How had he experienced the patient during the session? How he reacted to the hug? We tried hard to avoid unfair presumption in our evaluation. However, we hypothesized that this new patient had difficulty understanding appropriate boundaries that he had felt like hugging his new therapist, and had done so, regardless of the boundaries inherent in the therapeutic frame. Again, this was only a preliminary theory, and my supervisee needed to wait until their next session to explore the hug more fully with the patient. My supervisee departed our supervision meeting less flustered, having had the space to process the unsettling interaction.

During their next session, my supervisee brought up the hug, and encouraged his patient to be curious about it. As we had suspected, his patient had grown up in a home where he had been exposed to a great deal of boundary confusion, which had left him unable to discern appropriate boundaries in certain interactions. My supervisee and his new patient spent most of the session discussing the patient's boundary confusion. When the patient left the session, he thanked my supervisee, and left his office without hugging him.

The propriety of hugs and other physical contact (such as a consoling touch on the arm) between therapists and patients is a common clinical dilemma. Just as any other uncertainty during treatment, each instance must be assessed individually, with attention to the unique dyad, the timing of the physical contact, and the clinicians' and patients' possible responses.

Unlike other clinical predicaments, the issue of personal touch carries some unique characteristics. Many studies have focused on the necessity of personal touch, particularly in infancy, for the development of healthy adult attachment and relationships. Although a review of the literature is beyond the scope of this book, it is important to note that personal touch has been shown to be critical to an infant's ability to establish appropriate bonds and attachments with others. Extending this concept to our work with adult patients, personal touch, when used appropriately, can be more therapeutic than an informed clinical intervention. At times, a well-considered touch can communicate better than words. We must be open to the healing nature that personal touch can provide in our clinical work, but we must always be mindful of the possible meanings of such contact, and we must always respond in the best interests of our patients.

For example, in Chapter 7, I described a hug that patient M and I shared during our final termination session. This hug communicated the power and strength of what we had shared in our years of work together. However, it also communicated, for the first time, that M had become able to experience a relationship with a woman that maintained appropriate boundaries; our hug demonstrated to him that he had been accepted and appreciated for who he was, and that he was now able to connect with women in a non-sexual manner.

A hug is a great gift—one size fits all, and it's easy to exchange.

—Unknown

Another patient cried inconsolably during our first session following the death of her mother. She described the horror of the experience, her feelings of emptiness, and her devastating sense of loss. Her grief was poignant, and I was afraid that I was going to begin to cry with her. At the end of the session, I stood up and we hugged. As I processed the exchange after the session, I was uncertain who had initiated the hug. I thought it had been my patient, but I also knew that I felt compelled to hug her many times during the session. "Perhaps the hug unfolded naturally and reciprocally as a human exchange," I thought. Upon arriving for our next session, she thanked me for the hug. I wanted to ask her who had initiated it. "Does it really matter that much? Stop being so neurotic, Jacquie," I thought to myself. She thanked me again and stated, "It was exactly what I needed in that moment." Feeling the power of our shared moment, I realized that in this instance it was unnecessary to assess the hug any further. It had, simply, *helped*.

These were appropriate hugs. Unfortunately, therapists also confront incidents in which hugs or personal touches communicate toxicity within the dyad. Responsible clinicians must thoroughly explore these exchanges, and assist their patients to articulate the feelings that they have first communicated through inappropriate action.

Patient F provides an excellent example. She had been referred to me by her son's therapist, and presented with a dramatic background narrative. She was in her late thirties and married, with two young sons and a third child due in three months. Her husband was engaged in an extramarital affair, and he spent at least three nights away from home each week. F had discovered the affair within one month of its beginning, and had confronted her husband, who had admitted his infidelity and declared that he wanted a divorce. Despite these events, F and her husband remained sexually intimate, and F had become pregnant a few months later. Her husband, enraged because F had assured him she had been taking birth control pills, pleaded with her to terminate the pregnancy. F had refused, and fantasized that her husband would return to her once their third child was born. I believe that F purposely became pregnant in an effort to keep her husband, although she never directly admitted this to me. Indeed, F was so remarkably alienated from her own feelings that I often wondered whether she was able to recognize the manipulative nature of the pregnancy.

During the mere six months of our treatment, F spent most sessions describing her dramatic exchanges with her husband. She also discussed her husband and his girlfriend; she clearly was obsessed with their relationship, and was nearly stalking them. She avoided any exploration of her feelings, preferring instead to cling to the notion that her husband would eventually leave his girlfriend and return to his family. This defensive fantasy was so well integrated that F was incapable of exploring alternative outcomes; the possibility that her husband would pursue the divorce and move in with his girlfriend was not accessible.

In addition, F's clinical presentation was completely incongruent with the content she discussed in our sessions. She was remarkably, though falsely, elated in almost every session, unconsciously protecting herself from the underlying depression and fear with which she struggled. After about five sessions, F began to punctuate her elated performances by hugging me as she arrived, saying, "Hello, Dr. Simon, so good to see you!" Her hugs felt perfunctory and inauthentic. F's resistance to acknowledging her feelings made it difficult for me even to formulate a hypothesis surrounding what these hugs might have actually communicated.

I allowed F to hug me for about four sessions, while I processed them and attempted to figure out their meaning. Finally, I decided simply to ask F what she thought they meant, and as I asked, I wondered whether she was capable of providing any clinically relevant explanation. "I just like you *sooo* much, and I want to show you how much by giving you a hug," she bubbled. Again, I sensed her disconnectedness, both from me and from her own feelings. During that same session, through the content of her derivatives she revealed feeling as though she were competing with the other woman. "Ah," I thought. "She is defending herself against having to compete with me, creating a 'bond' between us by hugging me." Because F remained incapable of recognizing the significance of her actions at this time, I chose instead to address her actions by establishing appropriate boundaries between us. She seemed a bit disappointed following our discussion, but she did respect the boundaries and refrained from hugging me.

In another instance, one of my supervisees had begun to work with a new patient, who had a long history of trauma, emotional neglect, and deprivation. At the close of their second session, the patient had hugged her, and like my other supervisee, she planned to explore the hug with her patient during their next session. Unfortunately, the next four sessions were filled with the patient's experience of an overwhelming outside crisis, and there was no opportunity to process the hug. The patient continued to end each session by hugging her clinician, who, by this time, had discovered the patient's tendency to hug *all* of her doctors: she had described hugging her dentist. With this opening, my supervisee began to be curious with her patient about what these hugs communicated. The patient, who was quite insightful, shared that she thought the health care professionals from whom she sought treatment wanted or deserved to be hugged. My supervisee and her patient explored the patient's own desire to be hugged, and wondered whether she placed her own needs onto these professionals, imagining that her desires were also theirs. The patient took ownership of her own needs, and agreed that she had been so emotionally deprived that she longed to be held. Through further exploration and discussion, my supervisee was able to help her patient understand other ways these needs could be addressed through their therapy that through the empathic listening, consistency, and availability of her therapist, the patient would eventually feel less deprived of emotional closeness. The patient was able to internalize this, and eventually the hugs stopped.

"I'm committed to being totally honest with her, and so far the result feels pretty authentic. And the hug is just one part of that it's no big deal. This is a touch deprived woman, and touch is a symbol of caring. Trust me, the hug represents agape, not lust."

"But Earnest, I believe you. I believe that's what the hug represents for you. But to her? What's it mean to her?"

—Irvin Yalom, *Lying on the Couch*

This year, one of my interns has been hugged or touched by her patients more often than any clinician I have ever known. At first we joked about it, and explored what each touch meant for each individual patient. I initially understood these touches as coincidental and reflective of the patients my intern had been assigned, rather than as incidents that she might have been evoking through her mode of relating. As time went on and more patients began to hug her, we started to use our supervision sessions to explore what she might be unconsciously communicating to her patients. What might she have been doing that created an atmosphere conducive to hugging?

This particular intern is exceptionally warm, genuine, and engaging, and these traits had made her stand out among the other applicants during the internship interviewing process. There was an ease and comfort to her way of being, a natural and honest mode of interaction that was quite appealing, which continued throughout her internship. We began to explore together how her natural way of being-in-the-world might elicit a patient's desire for physical closeness with her. She became anxious as we explored this, and worried that she had done something wrong. I reassured her that she was not at fault, and that her personality was actually quite a gift because of this innate relational skill, she was able to engage challenging and interpersonally compromised patients. We began to work on ways that she might set firmer boundaries with her patients. She was not uncomfortable with the hugs, but we both knew that helping the patients articulate these symbolic communications would be more clinically corrective and helpful. We spent a number of months establishing appropriate techniques for each unique patient. It was tough work for both of us, but it was worth it in the end. Eventually, as she explored the hugs and the experientially and relationally relevant dynamics with her patients individually, each of them slowly became able to articulate the feelings that had prefaced their desires to hug her. This was major progress for my intern's patients, and a great opportunity for my intern to advance and develop her clinical skills. I was proud of her.

Chapter 9

Receiving Gifts

Let us spend one day as deliberately as Nature, and not be thrown off the track by every nutshell and mosquito's wing that falls on the rails.

—Henry David Thoreau, *Waldon and Other Writings*

It was the year of pies, we decided, ensconced in one of our intense intellectual discussions during the trauma case conference I facilitate. It was nearly Christmas, and we were discussing how to handle the complex experience of receiving gifts from patients. Three of the fourteen therapists that regularly attended the case conference had received a homemade pie from each of their respective patients. "Gifting" is more frequent during the holiday season, but it can occur at any time during the year. Each instance of "gifting" implies something different, and the timing of the gift, the nature of the gift, and the unique dyad between therapist and patient all must be considered when deciding whether or not to accept a gift. Whatever the distinctive circumstance, the therapist must understand, *a priori,* that each gift represents a type of metaphorical communication.

Regardless of our decision to accept or decline a gift, we must explore and understand the communication inherent in the giving. Ideally, it is best if this exploratory process happens before accepting or declining the symbolic overture. However, often the patients' experiences are unformulated, and their psychological processes are ill defined. While encouraging patients to be curious about their gift giving, I have often heard, "I just wanted to give you something." "I just saw this and thought of you" is another common comment. In these instances, we must respect where the patient is psychologically, and use our own hypotheses and clinical intuition to guide us to our decisions. The patient will likely have access to their unique feelings surrounding the experience, and the attendant capacity to process his or her gifting activity later in treatment.

As with the many other ambiguous predicaments clinicians often face, there is no easy or consistent answer here. We must assess our responses based on each unique dyad; however, as should be clear from the case narratives in this volume, we never can be quite sure exactly what will happen. We do commonly feel that our patients will experience our not accepting their gifts as personal rejections. Often, we accept gifts simply to avoid having to deal with what we believe will be our patients' negative feelings. This may be justifiable in many circumstances, but paradoxically, this is not always the case. We should not base our decisions about accepting or declining gifts on our own anxieties surrounding patient's possible reactions. Rather, we should make our decisions based solely on what we believe to be in the best interests of each individual patient.

The existential therapist can overcome, so far as possible, his own tendency to straight-jacket the patient by subjectivity by admitting his own bias and limitations to start with. Once these are admitted, the phenomenological approach can be of great help, as many of us have discovered, in seeing and relating to the patient as he really is.

—Rollo May, *Psychology and the Human Dilemma*

Patient E

I received my first gift from a patient as an extern, while terminating treatment with my patients before beginning my internship. This was one of my first experiences of having to terminate with longer-term patients, and I was already experiencing the normal emotional turmoil that characterizes the termination process. In the midst of containing my own separation issues and feelings of loss, as well as those of my patients, E gave me a gift. I had been seeing E for two years in once-weekly therapy. He had a long history of tremendous loss, and had become quite attached to me. I had also started to sense some erotic transference just prior to the beginning of our termination process.

During our last session, E gave me a gold necklace and a card as a "good-bye present." I felt very conflicted about how to handle this. I was early in my training, and I did not have the confidence or clinical proficiency that comes from experience. In addition, only this one, final session remained to explore, process, and decide whether to accept the gift. I felt like excusing myself and running out of the session to ask my supervisor what to do. I also fantasized about simply running out of the room altogether, thus saving myself from having to deal with the separation and the quandary surrounding the gift.

As best as my limited experience would allow, I tried to explore the meaning of the gift with E. I also created space in the session for E to fantasize about what it would be like if I did not accept his gift. I sensed from our exchange that E would feel extremely hurt, and that his sense of loss as we terminated therapy would be exacerbated if I did not accept the necklace. I truly felt torn. It made me uncomfortable that he had selected a necklace as his gift. It didn't look expensive (which would have compounded the dilemma), but it felt somewhat romantically intimate. I privately ruminated for at least fifteen minutes while simultaneously attempting to listen to E. I rarely wear necklaces, which confused me even further, because he certainly hadn't chosen to give me a necklace because he had noticed my preference for them. I finally asked him what had made him choose a necklace. He responded, "I thought it would look nice on you, and I wanted to give you something special so you will always remember me." I decided then to accept the gift. I felt guilty not accepting it, and I also felt that it was important for E to imagine me wearing the necklace. Remembering all that we had accomplished together in therapy, I thanked him and graciously put the necklace on just moments before the end of our last session. I still have the necklace.

Patient V

V arrived to a session and handed me a bouquet of flowers. I put them down on my desk and hesitantly responded, "Thank you. What are these for?" She responded, "They are a thank you for everything you have done for me." I had been seeing V once weekly for about three years. It felt good to imagine that the flowers were a symbol of V's gratitude, but I sensed that they held a more unformulated significance. I thought back to our previous session, during which V, who had difficulty expressing anger without suffering from associated guilt, had conveyed irritation with me through the content of her displaced derivatives. V described annoyance towards a friend who she felt had abandoned her in a time of emotional need, and I believed her anger had to do with the two-week vacation from which I had just returned. I queried, "I wonder if you also feel abandoned by *me*, because I was unavailable to you for two weeks." "No, you were on vacation," V replied. "That's different."

I sensed that V was protecting me from her anger. I also understood her dynamics when it came to expressing anger directly towards the person who had angered her: anger first, then guilt. I sensed that the flowers represented V's unconscious need to amend the displaced anger she had expressed in our previous session. V had not yet reached the point in treatment where she was able to access her feelings; therefore, she communicated her guilt through action. I felt it was too soon to confront her or make an interpretive intervention, so I thanked her for the flowers and accepted them. About eight months later, when a similar situation arose in the dynamics between us, I was able to confront V. By this time, she was able to acknowledge and explore her anger towards me, as well as her associated guilt. That was the last time V brought me flowers. As she became able to communicate her guilt with words, she no longer needed to rely on action.

The unconscious seems to take delight in breaking through and breaking up exactly what we cling to most rigidly in our conscious thinking.

—Rollo May, *Psychology and the Human Dilemma*

Patient Q

She was my second high-paid escort. I have worked with quite a few sex workers. We had been seeing each other once a week for about a year and a half. In the first year of therapy, she had inundated me with provocative stories about her exchanges with her clients. She led quite an exotic life. She was often paid to take long weekend trips all over the country, and even had been flown to Europe occasionally. She made her own schedule, selected her own clients, and made an enormous amount of money. She prided herself on all of this early in treatment. "I am in total control," she often shared. I imagined from this statement and from her other nuances that her chosen profession helped her to play out a power dynamic with men. While respecting her identity as an escort, I slowly encouraged her to be curious about the nature of the power and control she felt in her role. She was able to acknowledge the importance of being in control with men, but was unable to associate this with any underlying dynamics. She could not connect her need for power with anything deep or significant.

As treatment progressed, she began to exhibit some shame surrounding her profession and to reveal her power dynamics with her father. I could sense her difficulty in processing her more latent affects. She often diverted eye contact when exposing her shame, and I noticed this with her. One session, she brought me a framed painting of a daffodil painted in soft, soothing colors, as well as a hammer and nail with which to hang it. Before I could process this gift with her, she placed the painting on the wall, directly facing the chair in which she sat each week, and started hammering away. Very curiously, I observed her behavior without stopping her. When she eventually sat in her chair, I sensed that she was relieved to have accomplished her task. We sat in silence for a moment as I waited for her to start. She stated, "Now I have something to focus on when I am discussing feelings that are uncomfortable." She continued, "Sometimes I can't look at you when I am sharing my thoughts. Now I can look at the picture instead." I wondered if the painting provided her with a way to dissociate from the content of her disclosures, and from her primitive affect states, which were becoming more conscious. I learned later in her treatment that this was indeed the case. I did leave the painting on the wall for her, and I noticed that she used it exactly as she intended to.

Patient D

Big chunky rings are my thing. I have an entire jewelry box just for my rings. I travel with them, and I enjoy searching for the perfect ring to complete my outfit for the day. I actually feel slightly undressed on the rare occasions that I forget to wear a ring. I used to wear one on each hand until I became engaged. Now I only wear one on my right hand.

I had been seeing D in therapy twice a week for approximately two years when I became engaged. He was twenty-five years my senior, in great shape, and had an affinity for younger women. Occasionally, he would describe erotic fantasies that involved me. I would try to explore them, but D's defensive structure was very rigid, and he was inclined to black-and-white thinking. He often responded to questions by saying "It is what it is," which made him very difficult to work with.

Upon my engagement, he noticed my ring immediately. I tried to explore his feelings about this unintentional disclosure on my part, but he merely congratulated me, and claimed to have no feelings about my engagement. I felt envy and hostility in the room as D became increasingly irritable as the session progressed. D arrived to our following session with two small plastic rings for me. It was clear to me that he felt that he had competition, now. Throughout the session, I tried to explore the symbolic meaning of D's giving me rings in conjunction with his learning that I was engaged, but he wouldn't budge. I decided to accept the rings, and thanked D graciously; I was genuinely afraid that he would feel even more rejected if I declined his overture.

A few months later, D asked me to refer him to a different therapist. I tried to explore what was happening, and D emphatically declared, "You have your own things going on now. I just don't want to see you anymore!" I knew D could not tolerate his envy, or imagine a man in my life who was more important than he was. His defenses were so rigid that I knew any attempt to explore further would leave us both frustrated. I referred him to a colleague, and I regretfully admit that I experienced a sense of relief upon his departure.

Patient N

One of my supervisees arrived at our supervision session anxious, flustered, and disconcerted. She had been seeing her patient, N, in twice-weekly therapy for approximately one year. N was in her early forties, and was working on recovering from what she described as a "serious sex addiction." For weeks, we had been focusing on N in our supervision almost exclusively, because she related to her therapist (my supervisee) quite provocatively. My supervisee was gifted at forming alliances with challenging patients, and it appeared through our work together that N was beginning to relate to her in a more trusting and genuine manner. N currently resolved her "sex addiction" by abstaining from sexual relations entirely.

This day, my supervisee was bewildered, because N had brought her a book about sex addiction and stated, "I want you to read this. I think you will like it." My astute supervisee sensed that N imagined her also to be a recovering "sex addict." My supervisee, panicked by the nature of the gift as well as by her intuitive thoughts surrounding her patient's intention, accepted the book without processing it with N. She came to supervision and was very self-effacing. "These things happen, you were caught off guard," I explained. "Besides, N has a way of unnerving you to the point that you lose your ability to think clearly and clinically," I added.

My supervisee, feeling more in control of her own feelings, brought the book up in her next session with N. She explored the meaning of the gift with N, and also inquired about what N had hoped she would get out of reading it. N repeated, "I think you will like it." My supervisee was very uncomfortable with this remark, through which N silently provoked her by suggesting that they shared the same problem. "I am wondering if you believe I also suffer from 'sex addiction'," my supervisee bravely confronted N. "Don't you?" N winked. "You seem to understand me so well. This book helped me. I thought it would help you too." My supervisee did not disclose that she was not, in fact, a "sex addict," but rather explored with N why she might need to see her therapist as struggling with a similar issue. My supervisee did accept the book, and even decided to read it. At a later point in the treatment, she and N collaboratively concluded that N's imagining her therapist to have the same problem had helped reduce N's shame surrounding her "sex addiction."

Truly successful decision-making relies on a balance between deliberate and instinctive thinking.

—Malcolm Gladwell, *Blink*

I have received many small gifts from my patients over the years. Cups of coffee, cards, pens, magazine articles, and chocolate are some of the most common. Usually, I accept these gifts, explore their significance, examine the gift-giving overture, try to understand the underlying communication, and decipher what my accepting these gifts might mean to my patients.

We ate those homemade pies that my students had received from their patients, and we continued to discuss the propriety of accepting them during our case conference meeting. Each therapist who had been offered a pie had accepted, but only after exploring the possible implications of each gift with their patients. They were tasty pies, we all conceded, attempting to lighten the intensity of our clinical discussion, and, not immune from participating in unconscious, symbolic action of our own, we devoured the objects of our anxiety.

Chapter 10

Close Encounters with Patients Outside of the Session

I am a horrible singer. My sister and my cousin got all the musical talent in the family. But I do love karaoke. One night, feeling fancy and free, I convinced a few of my similarly impaired friends to join me at a local karaoke bar. "Come on! It'll be fun!" I pleaded. So off we went. We were having a great time, dancing and singing along with the other karaokers, when I got up the courage to perform my one song "Closer to Fine," by the Indigo Girls. I was on stage, having a great time. My friends were cheering me on. And then, to my consternation, I saw a patient laughing and clapping in the audience. Fortunately, I had been seeing this patient twice weekly for over two years, and we shared an exceptionally good rapport. Still, my knees locked and my legs felt slightly weak. Somehow, I finished my performance. I stepped down from the stage, and my patient walked over. "Good job, Doc," she remarked jovially. "Thank you," I replied, half-smiling. I was uncomfortable, but because of our unique dyad, I was also amused, and I knew she was too. At our next session, she teasingly asked, "So you switching careers on me?" I smiled at her and just shook my head, thinking, "This is the life of a therapist. You just never know what is going to happen."

One beautiful spring afternoon, I walked to work invigorated by a great run earlier that, morning when I spotted another patient holding hands with a man as they were walking down the street in a beeline straight towards me. This patient had entered therapy to process his fears about fully committing to his girlfriend, who had wanted to be married. He had never shared his interest in men with me, and yet here he was, right in front of me, holding hands with a man. He stopped me, and, to my surprise, casually introduced me to his "friend" as his therapist. We exchanged acknowledgments and off I went. I was confused. "No uneasiness, no consternation, just 'Hi, this is my friend'," I thought. I was baffled by his seeming lack of anxiety, but I was not shocked; after many years of this work, it takes a lot to surprise me. The patient came to our following session and said nothing about our meeting. I let the session progress, and then I finally asked him if he had any thoughts about our having seen each other on that day. "I'm glad you got to meet my lover," he responded. "Now you know why I am so confused." "Okay," I thought. "This *laissez-faire* response is kind of shocking. Wow, I have my work cut out for me."

There are no absolutes for something so relative as a human life. There are no rules for something so gentle as a human heart.

—Hugh Prather, *Notes to Myself*

I was sitting in a case conference relatively early in my training, when a senior psychologist began to share a serendipitous encounter with a patient outside of session. She had been having brunch the previous Saturday with her mother and brother at a small, popular restaurant when her patient had walked in. My colleague became quite anxious upon seeing her patient, and the hostess had intensified the situation by seating her patient and her friend directly adjacent to my colleague and her family. The restaurant was very small, and the tables were nearly on top of each other. My colleague could not ethically disclose to her mother and brother that one of the people seated next to them was her patient, and the patient did not acknowledge my colleague as her therapist. Our code of ethics forbids us from acknowledging our patients outside of session, unless they recognize us first. As a result, my colleague had no choice but to continue her meal while seated next to her patient, and because of the proximity of their seating, her patient was afforded complete access to the conversation among my colleague and her family members. I speechlessly listened to this story, and wondered how long it would be before I found myself grappling with a similar chance encounter. Considering the very short distance between my apartment and my office, I knew it was inevitable; unexpectedly meeting a patient in the outside world wasn't a matter of if, but of when, I thought.

More recently, while I was facilitating a trauma case conference, another of my colleagues used the metaphor of a video game to describe the therapeutic process. We psychologists love metaphors. She explained that patients often return thematically to a previous discussion as the therapy progresses, just as players of video games often return to previous levels as the game progresses but each time they return, they have a better understanding of how to navigate the terrain. The group and I found this to be a remarkably accurate metaphor for the therapeutic process. I would add that each level of the game remains unknown and unpredictable until the player encounters it for the first time. Responding quickly, yet appropriately, to unexpected occurrences in our sessions trains us for being surprised by chance meetings with patients outside of session; however, each encounter is different, and the unpredictability and awkwardness of these meetings can often leave us floundering for our clinical prowess and expertise.

Myths are a wonderful source of learning about the paradoxical, multidimensional, complex aspects of human nature.

—M. Scott Peck, *Further Along the Road Less Traveled*

My first chance encounter with a patient occurred in the supermarket not far from my apartment. The patient, P, was a woman twenty years my senior. She had been seeing me in once-weekly therapy for about four months. P was in treatment for her dysphoric mood, which surrounded a contentious relationship with her daughter, who was just about my age. I had quickly stopped at the supermarket to find a greeting card. I was unshowered, braless, and with my parents, who were leisurely walking about half a block behind me. I ran into the market and nearly into my patient, who stood at the front door selecting a shopping cart. She appeared delighted to see me, and enthusiastically exclaimed, "Hi, Dr. Simon! How are you?" I could only think that my parents could come strolling in at any moment. "This is not good," I anxiously thought. I didn't want to dismiss my patient. She was a very lonely woman, and seemed so happy to see a familiar face. So I simply responded, "Hi, nice to see you. Do you know if they have cards here?" She replied that they didn't, and directed me to a nearby card store. I thanked her, and practically sprinted out just in time to meet my parents at the front door of the market. "Whew," I thought, my heart still racing. "That was quite an experience. Thank goodness my parents were walking slowly." I then realized, "I'm not even wearing a bra. I hope she didn't notice."

During my training as an intern, I was taught that we must think as psychologists both in and out of the office. I wondered about how much we were allowed to "be human." After this encounter with P, I found myself wondering whether my career choice now demanded that I always wear a bra, even though I don't really need one. I went back and forth with this dilemma every time I left my apartment for days after running into P. I had never thought about my underwear so much in my life. It was exhausting and absurd. At our next session, my patient immediately discussed having seen me outside of the office. She stated, "It was nice to see that you have a life outside of your work." I thought this was generous of her. She was giving me permission to be fully human, rather than just a professional whose sole purpose was to act as her clinician.

Seeing patients outside of session, and the countless interactions that may result, are exceedingly unpredictable. I hear many anxieties surrounding this clinical likelihood from my supervisees, particularly when they have patients who live near them or who frequent the same establishments. As with all other clinically relevant issues, the nature of the unique dyad often informs the outcome of the encounter. Complicating this already multifaceted and unpredictable experience is the realization that sometimes patients see us without our knowledge. We often hear that this may have happened in the derivatives of their disclosures.

For example, one of my supervisees had been working with a quite difficult, eating-disordered patient for approximately six months. This patient, who also suffered from severe interpersonal issues, which often characterize patients with disordered eating, enjoyed sadistically provoking my supervisee, who worked inordinately hard to establish a working alliance with this patient. Her patient, who lived nearly around the corner from her, began alluding to the possibility that she had seen my supervisee in their neighborhood; she began to talk about going places that my supervisee frequented, such as Whole Foods. My supervisee, who is exceptionally intuitive, began to believe that the patient had indeed seen her in the market. However, the patient never disclosed that she actually had, and we thought it best at that point in treatment not to ask her. My supervisee remains anxious and self-conscious; she describes feeling she is on the lookout whenever she is in a place where it is likely that she and her patient may cross paths. "Ah, the life of a therapist," she sighed in our last supervision meeting.

A similar interaction occurred with patient D, who I had been seeing once a week for three years. She was primarily in treatment for generalized anxiety and panic attacks, although she also presented with body image issues. On this day, she disclosed to me that she had seen me running that morning as she was riding by in a car. She described envy surrounding her newfound knowledge that I exercised, stating, "So that's how you stay so thin. I wish I had the motivation to exercise."

Additionally, one of my supervisees had been seeing a patient once a week for approximately one year. One day, when my supervisee had gone to get his hair cut, he saw his patient leaving the building above his hairstylist's. Anxious that his patient might see him, he practically ran around the corner and hid, waiting for her to pass. Once he saw her walk down the street, he quickly snuck into the salon. Later that evening, he checked his records for his patient's address. To his dismay, he learned that she lived above the salon. My supervisee was convinced that she had seen him there before. "She must have," he stated, shocked and discomfited. My supervisee eventually switched salons.

One of the most striking encounters I have had with a patient outside of session occurred in August 2003, on the evening that the entire East Coast suffered an electrical black out. It was unbelievably hot, and I was wearing as little clothing as possible: a tube top, short shorts, and flip-flops. I also had my contacts lenses in (I usually wear my glasses when seeing patients). I was with one of my oldest friends and her new partner, who had remarkably made it into Manhattan from New Jersey, and we were supposed to attend the Indigo Girls' concert in Central Park that night. Uncertain if they would still be performing, and without cell phone service, we patiently waited in line to use a pay phone. We were all drinking beer, and my friend and her new girlfriend were publicly displaying their affection, when the woman on the phone finished her call, turned around, looked right at me, and stated, "Well, *hello*, Dr. Simon." She looked me up and down as I stood there feeling naked, exposed, and speechless. "You look great!" she said, but I sensed hostility in her tone. She called the following week and cancelled our session. In fact, she cancelled our therapy entirely, stating that she required "an older, more mature therapist." I had only been seeing her for about six weeks, and was unsure what to do. I encouraged her to come in to explore her feelings surrounding having seen me outside of the context of my professional role. She declined, and I never heard from her again.

We are guaranteed winners once we simply realize that everything that happens to us has been designed to teach us what we need to know on our journey.

—M. Scott Peck, *Further Along the Road Less Traveled*

Chapter 11

Self-Disclosure Responding to Patients' Personal Questions

Reveal yourself to the extent that it will be helpful to your patient; but if you want to stay in practice, have a care about how your self-disclosure will sound to other therapists.

—Irvin Yalom, *Lying on the Couch*

I was well beyond the appropriate age to be riding a razor scooter to work in a torrential rainstorm. A lifelong dancer, runner, and athlete, I considered myself invincible, so off I went. I had gone only about three blocks when the scooter got stuck in a pothole, flipped out from under me, and catapulted me directly to the middle of a busy New York City street, where I unglamorously landed. A UPS driver came rushing over and helped me up. "I'm okay," I insisted, though my ankle had twisted my leg into a clearly unnatural position. The pain was so intense that I couldn't even stand on my good leg, and the UPS driver had to carry me to the corner deli. A kind man in the deli hailed a cab, picked me up like a baby, put me in the cab, and told the driver to get me to the nearest emergency room.

Through a series of X-rays, the doctors discovered that my ankle was broken in two places, the ligaments were torn, and I needed emergency surgery. I was shaken by the accident and in excruciating pain, but soon, a morphine drip made me feel much better. I thought I was lucid and coherent (I was "feeling no pain"), however, I found out later from my friends and family that it had been clear to them that I was medicated, and that I had been slurring my words, when I called to tell them what happened. The surgeon had informed me that I would be in the hospital for at least three days, and suggested that I take the following week off from work. "You really did a number on yourself, and you are going to be in quite a bit of pain for at least ten days," he said, and I realized that I would have to call my patients. "Ugh," I thought, in a stupor. "How am I going to handle this one?"

"Should I disclose the truth?" I thought. "Well, I am going to be in a soft cast for at least six weeks, so I might as well be honest from the start. I can deal with the aftermath when I am no longer loaded up on painkillers and am feeling better," I concluded. So, forgetting that I was loaded up on painkillers (because I was loaded up on painkillers), I proceeded to call my patients. I informed them that I was fine, but that I had broken my ankle and would be out of the office for two weeks. I quickly contacted a colleague who agreed to cover for me, and I gave the patients her contact information.

This is a dramatic example, but it does demonstrate the kinds of stressful conditions under which therapists must sometimes contemplate how much of their personal lives to expose to their patients. Even as I prepared to return to work, I considered how many details would be appropriate to share. "Should I share that I was commuting via razor scooter? Should I apologize for making my cancellation calls during a morphine coma?" I wondered. When responding to personal questions, I always consider each unique patient/therapist dyad, the current status of treatment, and what certain disclosures might mean to each individual. Careful therapists must process both the content of their disclosures as well as the action of disclosing itself before revealing personal details to their patients.

Patients, naturally, are curious about us. We participate in formal, yet intense and intimate relationships with them, and become fixtures in their worlds. They create ideas, images, and fantasies about us, and about our lives outside of the therapy room. Some patients will directly ask personal questions, some will reveal their curiosity only beneath the surface of what they say, and others will say nothing at all. In each situation, the therapist must assess the propriety of disclosing personal information.

The concept of self-disclosure goes back to Freud's early writings, particularly his discussion of the concept of transference. Classical psychoanalysts assert that personal disclosure often interferes with the exploration of patients' fantasies, as well as with their transference of feelings onto the analyst, who should remain neutral and unknown. However, contemporary analysts and therapists have begun to understand transference as part of a co-created process, and even find self-disclosure or responses to inquires to be valuable tools in the therapeutic process.

When I first began practicing therapy, my grandmother told me about her only therapeutic experience. She had been seeing a psychiatrist for therapy once a week for about three months, and she had wanted to share a joke with him that she felt he might appreciate more if he were Jewish, so she asked him, "Are you Jewish?" Her therapist deflected the question and did not answer her, which left my grandmother feeling dehumanized and devalued. She left the office and never returned to therapy with him or any other therapist. If her therapist had explored the significance of her question, he might have learned the importance my grandmother placed on her Jewish identity, and that she was merely trying to relate to him so that they might establish a trusting alliance. Instead, my grandmother experienced his deflection of her question as a rejection of a fundamental part of herself. If this therapist had been more flexible in his thinking, he might have responded, "I will answer that question, but first help me understand what it means to you to know this about me." Perhaps if he had responded in such a way, my grandmother might not have needed his answer after all.

"That's wonderful. Same teacher?"
"Yes, same teacher, same class."
"You mean a still-life class?"
"You're hoping not, I think. Obviously there's something you're not sharing."
"Like what?" I began to feel uncomfortable. "What's your hunch?"
"I see I've hit on something." Irene grinned. "Almost never do you fall back on the traditional shrink practice of answering a question with a question."

—Irvin Yalom, *Momma and the Meaning of Life: Tales of Psychotherapy*

There are three distinct types of self-disclosure. The first type includes disclosure in response to a direct question asked by a patient, as well as the revelation of material about oneself or one's life. "Where are you going on vacation, Jacquie?" I am often asked. "I like that shirt. Where did you get it?" "Are you married? What does your husband do?" The dynamic becomes more complex when patients ask for direct advice: "What do you think about that?" or "What should I do?" Regardless of the relative simplicity or complexity of an inquiry, I always encourage patients to explore and be curious about why they are asking a particular question. My decision about answering the inquiry then depends on our unique dyad.

Patient B

Patient B was very promiscuous. She often had sexual liaisons with three to four men in a week, sometimes with two men simultaneously. "Double the pleasure," she would say. She described enjoying these encounters, and reflected no dystonic or uncomfortable feelings surrounding her behavior. "I am a sexual woman," she would announce. I sensed that she rationalized her decision to have multiple partners, but I held back from any inquiry, because she held firm to her perception of herself as "sexual." After a few months, she began to ask, "Dr. Simon, do you do that? Do you have sex with many different men? Have you ever had a threesome?" I felt backed against a wall. I understood that these questions reflected her disowned feelings of shame, and the discomfort she had split apart from her conscious self. In this situation, I thought it best to use her curiosity as a catalyst for encouraging her to question her own thoughts about herself and her behavior. "I am wondering why you would be interested in my sex life," I queried. She paused. "I want to know if you think what I am doing is okay?" she responded. "Are you uncomfortable with your lifestyle? You've never shared that before." I probed further. "Sometimes I am. I mean, I really want a relationship," she admitted. In this instance, my not answering B's questions had forced her to begin taking ownership of the parts of herself she had split off.

Patient M

"Wow, Jacquie, I love the tattoo on your foot," patient M commented. "What does it mean?" This patient also had a few tattoos, and I sensed that her noticing and asking about my tattoo was a way of relating to me. I felt that this patient, early in her treatment, would experience my deflection of this question as a dismissal, so I answered, "It means 'athlete' in Japanese." "I love that you have a tattoo," she replied. Later in our work together, I learned that her parents hated tattoos and often made demeaning comments about her decision to have them. Answering her questions had facilitated greater rapport between us, by implying a sense of acceptance.

Patient R

One of my supervisees was about to be married. She would be taking two weeks off for her honeymoon and would be returning to work with a different surname. She was very concerned about how much of her personal life to disclose to her patients, while still addressing these obvious changes to her schedule and to her publicly established identity. Before leaving, should she disclose where she would be, and explain that in two weeks, her name would be different? Or should she process this information with her patients upon her return? She was particularly distressed about how one patient might react. This patient desired a romantic relationship of her own, and had made both overt and covert comments indicating that she envied my supervisee's engagement ring. We explored the different possibilities for many weeks, profoundly aware of the effects this information could have on her patients, regardless of the timing of her disclosure. After many supervisions and discussions with her own therapist, she decided to disclose her impending marriage and name change prior to her departure. We felt that giving her patients five weeks to process the information before she left would reflect more empathy and reciprocity within the therapeutic relationships.

Patient C

I had been seeing patient C twice weekly for about two years when she began to discuss her issues of abandonment. C had been adopted, and her adoptive parents were emotionally abusive. In one session, she described excessive anxiety whenever she had to wait too long for someone, and as an example described often waiting up to thirty minutes for her sister to pick her up from the airport. I received a cancellation immediately before my next session with C, and, suffering from the onset of a cold, used the time to take a brief nap on the couch in my office. Having fallen into a much deeper sleep than I anticipated, I woke up and found myself fifteen minutes late for our appointment. I was beside myself. How could I have let this happen, especially after what C had shared with me two days ago? When she came into our session, she was crying hysterically. She imagined that I had been purposely late because of what she had told me at our last meeting. "Is this some kind of sick therapy technique?" she exclaimed, alarmed and angry. This was quite a predicament. With pillow impressions still on my face, I had to decide very quickly whether to reveal the truth. I decided to explore with C why she would imagine I would intentionally hurt her and betray her trust. She began to discuss the many manipulations and violations to which she had become victim in the past. Allowing space for her to process her anger towards me and the associated trust issues between us, I then told her the truth. She thanked me for being honest, and remarked, "Please don't let that happen again. I was in a panic waiting for you."

Later, still appalled by my own irresponsible actions, I consulted with a well-respected senior psychologist. We figured out that I had likely unconsciously responded to C's covertly expressed dependency issues by oversleeping. Then the senior psychologist reassured me that I was human, and that these things happened but she also pointedly remarked, "Get an alarm clock." I did, and I never overslept again.

The second type of self-disclosure involves clinicians' feelings during therapy, and whether these feelings should be shared with patients. This is a very tender and complex issue, because, as I have previously discussed, clinicians become the vessels into which patients often place their unconscious feelings, through projective identification or enactment, for example. However, through processing the feelings that our patients elicit from us during the co-created therapeutic process, we can profoundly help our patients identify and articulate their own feelings. If we perform interventions correctly and at the right times, disclosing our feelings can move the therapy forward, and also can establish greater relatedness between us and our patients.

Patient P

P seemed very disorganized upon her arrival at one of our sessions. She was remarkably tangential, appeared agitated, and began to discuss anger towards a friend, in keeping with her usual difficulty in expressing anger directly towards the person who had upset her. As the session continued and her thoughts remained disorganized, I started to sense that P was angry with *me*. She had called earlier in the week in a sort of crisis, and it had taken me four hours to call her back. She felt dismissed and unimportant, I thought; I could hear it in the content of her derivatives, and I felt it in the room. I gently remarked to P that I sensed that she was angry with me. She replied, "Yes, I am! I called you, and it took you all day to call me back. I was sitting by the phone all day waiting to talk with you!" I acknowledged and empathized with her experience. We then processed what it was like for her to share that she felt angry with me directly, rather than sharing with a third, uninvolved party. She responded, "It feels good, and thank you for validating my feelings." I was proud of her; this was progress

Patient J

One of my supervisees had been seeing J for three years. J had presented with significant marital discord and a long history of childhood sexual trauma. J's therapeutic relationship with my supervisee was her first relationship with a man that had appropriate boundaries. As their treatment unfolded, J's appreciation for the respect and unconditional support my supervisee provided became clear through the content of her dreams and derivatives. During one supervision session, my supervisee shared that J, distraught about the difficulties with her husband, had cried during their last session. My supervisee further informed me that in that moment, he had felt like hugging her. We discussed whether he should disclose this feeling to her, and he decided that he would bring it up during an appropriate opening in their following session. When he shared with J his desire to hug her during her distress, she thought about what he said and immediately began crying. When he explored with her what these tears meant, she shared with him that she felt cared for and supported. She also explained that it felt good that a man who did not want sex from her wanted to hug her. Their therapeutic relationship, and J's trust in her clinician, grew because of my supervisee's disclosure.

Patient W

I had been seeing W twice a week for nearly a year. She was going through a rocky divorce that her husband had initiated, and was having an inordinately difficult time dealing with her feelings of rejection and abandonment. Her soon-to-be-ex-husband was already involved with another, much younger woman. W suspected that his decision to leave her had to do with this other woman, although he had never admitted it. He would say only that he simply wasn't in love with W anymore. In countless sessions, W would be on the verge of tears, but would quickly regain her composure and resort back to intellectualizing her feelings. During one session, she shared a painful exchange in which she had seen her soon-to-be-ex-husband walking down the street with his girlfriend. As she was replaying the events of their exchange, she looked as though she was about to cry, but stopped herself; W viewed herself as a strong woman who wouldn't let her ex make her cry. As she told her story, her psychic pain was poignant and filled the room so much so, that I found *myself* wanting to cry. "That sounds absolutely horrible and painful. I feel like crying," I shared. W began sobbing as she told me she felt humiliated by seeing her ex look so happy while she still miserably pined for him.

Patient B

Disclosing our feelings during therapy becomes even more complex when our patients evoke and provoke our anger within the therapeutic dyad. Sharing our feelings of anger is most therapeutically effective when undertaken within a firmly established alliance. Patients with extreme interpersonal difficulties can benefit remarkably from such revelations if we time them correctly.

Patient B entered therapy for help with her pervasive interpersonal deficiencies, which characterized all her relationships and promoted chaos throughout her life. She had contentious friendships, problems at work, and drama-ridden intimate relationships. After three years of therapy, which included my constant management of her turmoil and provocations within our therapeutic relationship, she finally began to question her own responsibility for the maintenance of her interpersonal problems. I liked B, but found her to be controlling, overbearing, and extremely entitled; she did evoke anger from me, and I often felt myself grinding my teeth during our sessions, to restrain my own aggressive feelings. During one grueling session in which she discussed conflict with a co-worker, she directly asked, "Jacquie, is it my fault? This just keeps happening." I decided to risk answering her, though I was uncertain where my answer would lead. "B," I gently replied, "There are times where I feel very controlled by you, and I become angry as a result." She looked down, and I became anxious as I awaited her response. "I am controlling, aren't I? That could make people angry? It has made you angry?" "Yes," I answered. "There are times when I feel angry and don't know how to respond to you without being attacked." She looked down again, and I asked how she felt about what I had just shared with her. B responded, "I'm sorry. I don't know how else to get people to hear me or meet my needs. Can I get better?" Delighted by her insight, I told her that because she had become aware of and had accepted her role in her personal exchanges, that we could now work hard to help her relate to people in a more congenial and reciprocal manner.

Patient D

The third type of disclosure involves therapists' unintentional self-revelations. Our patients consciously or unconsciously absorb and assess us constantly: our manner of dress, our unique methods of communication, our body language, our cadence, our eye contact, and even our office furniture provide windows into our personal lives.

I had only been seeing D for about two months. She described considerable discomfort with her body. She felt "fat," which was a self-image incongruent with her nearly perfect figure. She also shared notable envy towards other women. I used my own body as a therapeutic catalyst, by encouraging her to explore any feelings she may have had about sitting with me, a very thin, athletic woman. D brushed this off, and stated that she felt "fine." However, during one of our summertime sessions, my office was uncomfortably warm, and I removed my blazer, unthinkingly exposing my upper arms. D remarked immediately. "Dr. Simon, your arms are so toned. How did you get them to look like that? Is it from running? I saw you running on the street a few weeks ago." D had revealed earlier in our therapy that she was also a runner, and I could feel her envy permeating the room. I responded, "Is it uncomfortable for you to see my arms? Are you comparing your body to mine?" She replied that she was not, but I didn't believe her, and I scrambled to deflect the envy she wasn't ready to share by revealing that I also swam, in addition to running. I hoped this would give her an alternative explanation for my toned arms. D cancelled our next session, and then called the following week to say that she thought she could work through her issues on her own. I imagined that D was unable to sit with the envy she felt because it was so early in her treatment, and that she had abandoned therapy rather than confront her own feelings.

Patient G

I have been working with G twice weekly for seven years. When we began our treatment, she reacted strongly to my appearance. G is thirty years my senior. She arrives to our sessions impeccably and expensively dressed, and perfectly made-up and coiffed. Early in our therapy, she revealed that my more bohemian personal style irritated and provoked her, by making very direct, devaluing comments about my appearance. "You need highlights. Why don't you wear makeup? You are never going to meet a husband looking as you do," she would constantly remark. During one session, she gave me a backhanded compliment, noticing, "Your hair looks good today. What did you do different? It usually looks greasy." She would often bring beauty magazines to therapy, and encourage me to buy makeup and beauty products. We spent at least two years exploring what my appearance meant to her and why it seemed to bother her so much. As treatment progressed and we were finally able to establish a comfortable rapport, G disclosed that she felt injured by my lack of response to her comments, and wondered why I hadn't taken any of her beauty advice. She painfully disclosed that she had been beautiful when she was younger, and that at that time in her life, many women had sought her out for beauty advice, because they had wanted to look like her. It injured her that I hadn't responded in the same way. G profoundly identified herself through her appearance, and aging was inordinately difficult for her. We worked hard to help her recognize unique inner qualities and strengths that had nothing to do with age or physical appearance. Now, more comfortable with herself, G often genuinely compliments my style, hair, and overall appearance.

*   *   *

One morning, I was in the middle of scheduling an initial appointment with a new patient when my cat sat purposefully on my appointment book. I excused myself from the phone call for a moment to shoo my cat away, and I returned to the phone, appointment book in hand. After four months of treating this patient, she shared with me that she had known that we would be a good match during that first phone call. She smiled as she revealed that she had heard me talking to my cat, and she knew in that moment that I was "quirky." "I liked that," she said.

Index

28995903R00069

Made in the USA
Lexington, KY
09 January 2014